My One True Father

Diane "Broken Arrow" Leeward

Copyright © 2019 Diane "Broken Arrow" Leeward

All rights reserved. No part of this publication may be reproduced, distributed, or transmitted in any form or by any means, including photocopying, recording, or other electronic or mechanical methods, without the prior written permission of the publisher, except in the case of brief quotations embodied in critical reviews and certain other noncommercial uses permitted by copyright law.

ISBN-13: 978-1-951300-86-9

Liberation's Publishing LLC
West Point, Mississippi
www.liberationspublishing.com

My One True Father

Diane "Broken Arrow" Leeward

Dedication

This book is dedicated to Jesus Christ my Lord and Savior. Without him I am nothing! My relationship with him changed everything in my life! If God is writing your story, everything is possible for you. We are here to create, we are ambassadors for Christ so, this is my story and what God did in my life. God is good and God set me free. God used my deepest wounds to help you to tell your story too. Pay it forward and set them free. Freedom leads to joy. I also dedicate this book to my husband and my kids who stood beside me through it all and my grandmother and my Aunt and Uncle who held me tight when I needed it the most in my life and made me feel loved. Last and not least, I dedicate this book to Pastor Doug from Calvary Chapel, of Fort Lauderdale Florida. "We all have a story to tell!"

Thank You.

Table of Content

Contents

By Grace I Stand 9

The Start 17

Barry 23

More Moves 35

Freedom 41

More Changes 57

Nothing Again 65

God's Help 81

Back to Florida 99

God's Kindness 123

My Turnaround 161

Appendix 173

Diane "Broken Arrow" Leeward

By Grace I Stand

Grace means all your mistakes now serve a purpose instead of serving shame.

Grace changes everything, For by Grace I have been saved through faith in The Lord Jesus Christ. It's a gift from God, not a result from works. I thought I was broken beyond repair and if you see anything different, it's only by the grace of God. I'm telling this story simply because there are so many other people out there in this world who live with the shame that I have all my life. No one to talk to or trust with my life's secrets. Some secrets aren't even mine but became mine not to tell. I felt isolated and fear consumed me my whole life.

I'm here to tell you, you're not alone. I'm no longer afraid. Give it to God put it all in his hands and he'll take care of all your cares, wants, and needs. I was blessed with a large family and I still felt alone. Every day is a struggle, but I have God almighty on my side to guide me and take care of me when I fall.

God is giving me my song back!

In my years this is what I've learned. To live by faith means to Choose God's priorities over your own rather than enjoy the passing of sin. Connecting to God, it's eternal, and a relationship with Jesus changes everything. We are called to make God visible in our lives. Telling God's story doesn't just express joy it completes it. When you step into the light you find freedom. God loves to give us second chances at divine moments.

Take a leap of Faith! It starts with one step. If you choose to remember divine moments, don't forget them write them down so you don't forget. It's never too late to get it right with God. The enemy will use deceit and lies to stop you from taking ground. Prayer opens our minds to see the truth and God's love. Here are a few notes I took in church just to remind me that God's love can bring you through anything.

Love requires a response:
1) Love reveals the real you.
2) Love grows us in God's family
3) Real love must be fought for
4) Perfect love exposes lie
5) Perfect love is contagious
6) Perfect love drives fear out.
7) Perfect love dislodges hate.

Secrets: We all have them, Destruction of Secrets:

1) It doesn't just hurt you.
2) It won't stay secret
3) The hardest lie to see is the lie to yourself.
4) Your secret sin will show up in your future. You need to confess.
5) Burying your secret is destructive to your soul.

Let's not forget about our failures; God knows we all have those.

Failures:

1) Fail back- Blame others
2) Fail forward-Take responsibility
3) Fail backward- Repeat the same mistake
4) Fail forward-embrace failure
5) Fail backward-avoid failure
6) Fail forward reverse
7) Failure isn't fatal- you can only hang your head so long.
8) Failure doesn't own you
9) Failure teaches us to listen.
10) Failure teaches us new approaches and teaches us the dangers of over confidence.
11) Failure leads us to victory.
12) Failure creates a holy dependency.

God can turn your failure into greatness! Love your God, love your neighbor. It's never too late to be who you could have been. God sends out broken people for his glory. There's only one hero in our story, his name is Jesus! There is no higher calling than to be a child of God. Let the values of the kingdom shape your values.

In God's kingdom, mercy triumphs over judgment. Never give up on your pursuit of God. Look for truth on the narrow road. Tell yourself the truth. An eternal mind set changes your life on earth and it's our temporary home. Heaven is eternity, it's a destination and our greatest desires are met there. Seeing God face to face will be our greatest joy! God is waiting for you to release control. In the mist of your unsolvable problems, focus on the Great problem solver. Even at your worst moment God's grace is still offered. He wants to redeem your pain with a promise.

Walking with God:

1) Limitless presents
2) Limitless promises
3) Limitless purpose
4) Limitless perspectives (Learning to see what God sees.
5) Limitless power (Love like God)
6) Limitless provisions (contentment and peace)

How to walk with God:

1) Decide to walk with God
2) Identify a destination
3) You must participate daily.

God's spirit is looking for a place to land, he commands us to take ground and occupy until he comes. God will meet us in our worship. God will keep his promise to you and his mercy triumphs over tribulation. We all share the same bloodline; you can be a part of a tribe without being tribal. When God is actively speaking there is a difference between hearing and listening.

1) Listen with your eyes.
2) Take technology breaks.
3) Practice the presence of God.
4) See what you cannot see.

We all have a story to tell. Your story like mine is full of God's blessings. Your story has tragedy and blessings. We may not see them but that just means you're not looking. If you trust the author of your story, you can worship in tragedy. God has more work to do in me, he has not abandoned me.

Diane "Broken Arrow" Leeward

PTSD is real! Some people will fail you, but God has a purpose for you and me. Sometimes the greater the suffering, the greater the glory. A good story can get into your soul. When tragedy strikes, look for redemption, look forward in hope! If you're not dead you're not done! We all have wounds and scars, but wounds heal, and scars remind. When you have faith then you believe in advance what will only make sense in reverse. Faith is homesickness for a place we've never been. There is no victory without battle. Remember: God is a giver and the world is a taker. Choosing God first makes everything second. Your choices create your destiny. Generosity is a choice, give with the heart of a child.

This story is based on a sad but true story but, God's love conquers no matter what.

My grandmother was my connection to God. She was the reason I can forgive my mother or any other person who has hurt me. I know God sent her to me for a reason. My life seems normal on the outside but on the inside, I am a mess! My grandmother taught me to love unconditionally and forgive no matter how bad things were.

It's the hardest thing I've tried to do, but with God's help she made everything bearable for me. My grandmother never spoke English, but she understood every word I ever spoke to her and I understood her even though I didn't speak Spanish. We had a very special bond that I know I'll never have again with anyone. She spoke to me with love and understanding like no other had before. She was my rock and my Angel, I miss her dearly, and I know she watches over me because I can feel her loving presence.

I've never known such a kind and loving spirit like hers and now that she's gone, my Aunt May, (who is most like her in my opinion) is the only one I know whom I can talk to and get almost the same kind of love and understanding from. My grandmother always hugged and kissed us and always made us feel loved. My mother was not so lovable to us but at the time we didn't know the difference because she left us with my grandmother a lot. Grandma showed us what love was and what it felt like. She is gone now but, before she left this earth, she handed me back over to God. Her job here was over and I'd like to think she did a good job.

Diane "Broken Arrow" Leeward

The Start

My first memories as a child were living with my grandmother. Grandma lived in a small adobe house and she had a disabled daughter who she also took care of. Her name was Mary, she was bound to a wheelchair her whole life due to a birth defect. Mary was a trooper and she endured a lot of pain and hospital stays. Despite her illness she and a couple of my other aunts were up to the task of helping my grandma with all of us.

I can remember we used an outhouse because there was no toilet in the house. At night grandma put a large gallon can in the kitchen, so if we had to go to the bathroom at night, we could go in that. We lived near the Mexican border, and it was very dangerous to be out at night, so the can in the kitchen was our bathroom at night. She had an old fashion pump in the kitchen for water. It was well water, and that's all we had.

When it came to bath time, she had a large washtub that she used to wash cloths in and doubled as a bathtub. Grandma would heat up the water on the gas stove and when the tub was half full of warm water, she would put us all in there at one time. We had a roof over our heads. Food in our bellies, clean clothes on our back, and a woman who loved us unconditionally.

I can't imagine taking on all that responsibility. She took care of us and worked in the kitchen of a small restaurant in town. The town was small, one or two restaurants, one small hotel, a grocery store, and even a movie theater. I think that the movie theater is the oldest one left in the country. It's been out of commission for years, but it's still standing today.

We went to the only school in town. Each grade only had a few students. It didn't have a cafeteria, so we walked home for lunch every day. We all slept in one big bed; boy they had their hands full!

I remember once a month going into town for the government issued food. That's where we were introduced to can meat, powdered milk, cheese etc.... We all went so we could help carry the food home.

Mom married dad, Daniel, when he was in the Air Force. She had three of us in two years' time, my oldest brother Neil, my-self, and my twin Daniel Jr. We moved to Indiana where the three of us were born. Indiana would become a place we came back to often. When dad had to report for duty mom took us back to Texas. He and my mother had one more child, her name was Ann. We apparently moved to San Antonio where Daniel was stationed at the time. Ann was born there, and not long after, mom and Daniel called it quits.

Later mom met and married a man named Luis. That relationship was short lived. She tried to make it work again with Daniel, but when he saw she was pregnant he said, "that's not mine." She left for a while and when mom came back to Daniel, she told him she had lost the baby. She had taken the baby, Leigh, to Luis and left her there. Luis was happy to have her.

The relationship failed again, and mom took us back to grandma's house. While there she started having health issues and tuberculosis was the culprit. It ran in her family health history. My grandfather and an uncle lost their battle with it before we were born. Mom only had to have a lung removed. She was in the hospital for over a year. Back then they kept you in the hospital for long periods of time.

While mom was in the hospital Dad tried to take us from my grandmother's home in Texas back to Indiana. Grandma and my aunts wouldn't let him. He called child services and complained that we were not in a clean and healthy environment and wanted custody. He ended up taking us back to Indiana, but when mom was able, she came to get us. I don't know the entire story I only have my moms' side to work with.

Diane "Broken Arrow" Leeward

Mom's marriage to my dad was over, and I didn't even remember him. I vaguely remembered another father when Mom came home with another baby! She was baby number six. My sister Leigh was left with her father Luis to raise and I didn't even miss her until we were a little older. I didn't even know her! Out of sight out of mind, I guess. We went back and forth to so many different homes.

My second dad Luis was once in the Army and played college football. He was also an alcoholic, and very abusive to my brothers. He was a barber and would cut my brothers hair in Mohawks and let people laugh at them. I don't really remember all this, but I was told this story by relatives. Apparently my last two sisters were his. (According to mom) Mom went back and forth with these two men she married.

When he married mom, he took us all to Oklahoma, his hometown. Again, we were taken away from our grandmother. My mom brought one of her cousins with us to help with taking care of us. This was when I first remember watching TV. It was a small black & white tv. I remember there was a funeral going on, and I didn't understand what that was at the time. I remember it was so sad. It was the funeral of our president John F. Kennedy in 1963.

My One True Father

The marriage didn't work out! Back to Texas without my sister Leigh. I think when I was 7 or 8 mom married husband three. His name was Barry. Barry was in the Army. He moved in with us and that's when I first remember calling someone daddy. Mom let him adopt us and he changed our last names. We never heard from our real dad again and it didn't matter anyway because I didn't remember him at all. Grandma's house is all I remember as a child where it was safe, and we were loved.

Pictures and stories from mom filled in the blanks. As we got older, we started to ask questions. I want you to always remember there are two sides to every story and we only heard one side. We believed mom because she was our mom and we trusted her completely. We had no reason not to. I remember Barry always made me feel uneasy, maybe because I was so confused about who he was!

I remember our first Christmas with him. We had his army socks hanging from the wall, he said they were our Christmas stockings, that's the first Christmas I remember. I didn't understand, but what I did understand is that they had candy in them and an orange at the bottom. I don't know why that stuck in my head, but it did.

Mom was pregnant again, and we ended up leaving Texas and moving to Florida. This was drastic! We were going to be so far from my grandma! We brought my Aunt May with us to help mom out with another baby on the way. Barry's parents lived in So Florida, and they were very upset that he married a woman with 6 kids (Leigh didn't live with us yet) and they doubted that the one mom was carrying was his.

Well, Barry was a red headed Irishman with a mean streak, and when my youngest sister was born, she had the most beautiful red hair I had ever seen! That's when his parents accepted mom, the rest of us, not so much. We were Mexican and Indian and whatever my real father was. They thought their son could have done better. He was in his twenties and mom was a couple of years older. She was twenty-nine when she had baby number seven with husband number three.

Now that I think about it, what parent wouldn't be upset! His first marriage and seven kids!

Barry

We moved into a house that wasn't big enough for all of us, so Barry added two more bedrooms to the other side of the house making it a five-bedroom house. Barry was an electrician by trade, and not a bad carpenter. My sister Leigh came back to live with us, and I was so happy I hated that I barely remembered her, and I didn't understand why she got to live with her father and the rest of us couldn't. Mom never talked about him to us, so I guess we were too young to understand. I guess out of sight out of mind. We had bigger fish to fry now. When my youngest sister Marie was six months old. My Mom went for her checkup and got the news that she had ovarian cancer. She ended up having a hysterectomy.

We had to cross a field in front of the house to the 7-11 to use a pay phone to talk to mom while she was in the hospital. We didn't have a phone yet. I thought we weren't going to see her again. We made sure we had plenty of dimes to put in the phone so we could each talk to her. The last time she went into a hospital we didn't see her for over a year. My Aunt took care of us until she came home.

She came home and, she started working again when she felt better. I met my first best friend ever, Michelle, and she lived next door. We did everything together! She would give me a ride to school on her bike and back home every day. I loved her so much. One day she asked if I could spend the night. I never did that before. We had a great time. Her parents took us out to eat and I use to be so scared because I didn't know how to act or what to order. I never went out to a real restaurant, so I just got what my friend Michelle got. We played games and stayed up late.

It felt so good to be away from home even just over night and next door. I still had to be home early, being the oldest girl, I had to watch my youngest sisters. We never went out to eat, because there was too many of us, so only my parents went out. My parents went out maybe once a week with their friends to a club to dance and listen to country music, or their friends would come to our house. Sometimes they would bring their kids.

They would play cards and drink for hours. They would drink a lot, and I knew what that meant. Barry always had to be the life of the party especially at our expense. We literally had to wait on him hand and foot. He would call us awful names like moron, a** hole, half breed, spick, etc. I couldn't stand him, and I always tried to stay out of his way. He always made us feel like we were no body's and we didn't matter. Mom never stood up for us, and so we believed it.

My One True Father

I remember one day asking mom, what was my real dad's nationality? And why haven't we heard from him, and why can't we go live with him? She said we were half Irish, because my real dad was, and he didn't want us. I believed her; I mean why not? She's my mom and I trusted and believed her. She would never lie about something like that! I never even questioned it! I used to wonder what I did to make him hate me and not want me anymore.

Barry was a mean drunk and was ugly to us with a belt or whatever he had handy. Usually mom wasn't home when he hit us. No one was safe either. He used to line us up and ask who did whatever he was angry about at the time. If no one spoke up, we would all get hit until someone confessed. That someone was usually Daniel. He always took one for the team. Barry really scared us all.

My sister Ann was the most stubborn and he use to hit her just to make her cry. Funny thing is when SHE got bored, she would cry just so she could go play. Me! I cried before I got hit! He put fear in me like no child should ever feel. One day we came home with report cards, and Daniel and I didn't do so well in math. Barry made us both drop our pants to our bare butts and bend over the bed. He would quiz us, and if we got the answer wrong, we got paddled. I really think he got off on that. I remember Daniel would hold my hand to comfort me. We would go without sitting for a long time, but we couldn't tell mom what he was doing because he would deny it and we would get it again after mom left for work. Mom always believed him over us. He sure knew how to control us.

Mom would make our lunches for school every day and give us a nickel for milk. It was rare to get to buy lunch, it was twenty-five-cents for each of us. If mom worked late, she would leave lunch money on the table for each of us. Aunt May worked days, and Barry worked days. Mom was home with the baby till her dinner shift at her job started. We didn't see mom much those days. By the time we were home my Aunt May took care of us.

I remember the big craze for Barry was the two-way radio. He used to talk to truckers all night long while he drank himself stupid. We would listen to that radio all night unless mom dragged him to bed. We were lucky those nights, because he left us alone.

We found a nice little church right behind the elementary school that we attended. We started to go there and found that the preacher there was also our gym teacher at school. We really liked it there, and we went every Sunday. That's where I first gave my life to Christ and was baptized. I remembered feeling so different, like I'd never felt. I wanted to keep going back. Little did I know it was the Holy Spirit. I didn't want to lose this feeling, so I felt like I had to live a good life so this wonderful feeling would last. That day my life was changed forever.

Mom didn't always go, and Barry never went. This house was known to me as the house of horrors where our nightmares began. One night before mom came home from work Barry came into our room butt naked! My two sisters and I shared a bedroom. We had a set of bunk beds and a single bed. I slept on the top. He scared me and I didn't know what he wanted or why he was there. I thank God that my Aunt heard him and came in to investigate (her room was next to ours). He said he heard a noise out of our window. His room was clear across the other side of the house. He smelled of beer and was totally disgusting.

The next day no one said a word. My Aunt and I didn't know what to do. The next night he went to my Aunts room, again butt naked and drunk. She pretended to be asleep, but she was scared to death. My mom found him and took him back to their room. It got to the point where we could hear his ankles cracking as he came walking across the house to our room. I think I slept with one eye open after that. Mom couldn't always save us, but when she did, she never asked if we were ok or what he was doing. She knew what he was doing but did nothing about it.

Diane "Broken Arrow" Leeward

I knew we were on our own. My sister Leigh used to cry and say OMG here he comes! I would pretend I thought it was my brothers playing around and yell at them to go back to bed and go to sleep. Mom would hear and come take him back to bed. Aunt May tried to tell mom what he was doing but to no avail. Mom didn't want to believe her, but Barry saw her as a threat and kicked her out. That's when the real nightmares began.

Without Aunt May in the house Barry did what he wanted to any time he wanted to. By the time mom got home from work everything was over. Mom thought he stopped messing with us. Mom worked dinner shift, so anytime he wanted one of us he would make everyone sit in front of the TV with a bowl of ice cream while he took who he wanted into his room to "rub his back".

My sisters and I knew exactly what that meant, and he always made Daniel rub his feet. He had the longest skinniest toes I've ever seen, and they were disgusting! By the time mom got home from her dinner shift everyone was sleeping and Barry was passed out and satisfied.

Outside of the house people saw us as "the Brady Bunch" but no one knew our dirty secrets. We played outside all day, climbed trees, made forts, and hung out with the neighborhood kids. We seemed like the all-

American family. The only time I was able to sleep well was when I spent the night with my friend Michelle. Michelle and her older sisters taught me all about my period and boys. Her parents and mine were good friends. I couldn't ever bring myself to tell my best friend what Barry was doing to us, because I was so ashamed and afraid of what would happen if anyone outside the family found out. My brothers didn't even know. Sometimes when I went to Michelle's house, I had to take my two youngest sisters with me because I was the oldest and I had to take care of them.

One day my parents told us we were moving to another home in a different neighborhood. We were very upset about that, but we had no choice. We adjusted and we finally got a phone in the house. I was able to call Michelle every now and then. My parents and my Aunt made up. Aunt May met a very nice guy and they ended up getting married. We were there only a couple of years before we moved back to Oklahoma. My mom's ex-husband Luis gave us his house to live in until we got settled and found something better.

Barry and Luis got along great. They would both drink themselves stupid. If Luis only knew what Barry was doing to his little girl, Luis would have killed Barry. Barry was on his best behavior while we were there, thank God. We had chickens, dogs, and horses. Daniel had a pony named Rachel. He loved that pony, and he was the only one who could ride her. She didn't like anyone else. He really had a way with animals.

One day Barry wanted to slaughter some chickens, because there were so many. He decided to throw them off the roof at us, and we had to catch them so he could kill them. Of course, Barry and Luis were both drunk and thought it was funny to terrorize us all. After we gathered them, he hung them upside down on the cloths line and proceeded to chop their heads off. The blood was everywhere! Then we had to eat them for dinner. I had nightmares for a long time.

Going back there was a total nightmare for my oldest brother Neil. Luis use to beat my brother often and severely when he was very young. My grandmother told me that she cried so much for him when she had to patch him up. Mom was in denial and said her first husband dropped Neil on his head while playing with him. I knew better. Mom is still in denial about that to this day.

We would go back to Texas every now and then to visit my grandmother, and it was like going to Disney. My cousins lived next door to my grandmother (another of my mom's sister and her family). My Aunts husband liked to drink too, so he and Barry got along just fine. We all used to hide when they both got drunk, because they both were stupid when drunk. We all knew what they were both capable of doing when this would happen. Mom and her sister would keep them away from us kids because they also knew what they would do to us kids when they've been drinking. My uncle liked to hit and of course we know what Barry liked to do, thankfully they both would pass out till the next day.

Back to Oklahoma, and we finally moved into another house. I think by then I was fourteen and in middle school. We had a basement in that house and the boys lived down there. Of course, me and my sisters shared a room; we were ok with that. We always shared a room. Mom and Aunt May worked at the same restaurant near an Air force base. There were a lot of soldiers in and out of that place.

Mom was very friendly with them all. They were all regulars. There was one guy who was a young tall blond who could get milk on base very cheap. It was so inexpensive on base, and he would get it for us. He always came over to the house to deliver it. He really got on my nerves. He used to pick fights with me all the time. I remember how bad he smelled all the time. Being a little more grown up now I realized he liked me and not in a good way. I tried to stay clear of him whenever he came over. I could never talk to mom about anything for fear she wouldn't believe me. By now I felt I always had to be on my guard.

One day, mom came home with this guy and announced he was going to stay with us for a while and I thought where was he going to sleep???? The house was already to capacity! I think Barry saw him as moving in on his turf, and not just because it was inappropriate or anything, don't know what mom was thinking!

When I turned fifteen, I got my first job working in a grocery store making donuts. I met my first ever boyfriend. He bagged groceries and, on his break, he would come talk to me. It didn't last (neither did the job) I was not ready for someone else putting his hands on me. He tried, and I wasn't having it. I had no one to talk to, so I kept a lot of things bottled up inside. I trusted NO ONE especially my own mother.

She didn't help me or my sisters with Barry, why would she help with anyone else? I did what was expected of me and stayed to myself. I felt like I was in my own private prison with no chance of being paroled any time soon. That year I learned to drive. I finally felt like I had independence. My mom got Daniel and I a job busing tables where she worked. We only worked on weekends. Daniel started training to cook, but they wouldn't give him a shift till he was sixteen.

When we turned sixteen, I got to wait tables and Daniel worked in the kitchen. The head cook asked me out, but mom told him to stay away from her daughter!! She acted like she cared but, I knew different. I thought he was cute! He had long hair and smoked cigarettes and pot. He was a bad boy and I found him interesting. He was everything my parents hated, but he was always was a gentleman to me. He never pushed himself on me.

I kept him at a distance for a long time. He was only eight months older than me and like any other guys I met I was afraid of him. He was married with a kid but was separated and lived with the graveyard cook. He was a wild child!

Ted's mother worked there too, and she, my Mom, and my Aunt were all friends and co-workers. My Uncle Joe also cooked at the same place. What a great guy he is. I was so happy when he and my Aunt May got married. She deserved to be happy. I love and trust them very much. I don't know where we would be without them in our lives.

Diane "Broken Arrow" Leeward

More Moves

After I turned sixteen Barry moved us yet again ten miles away from my school. We had to change schools again!! I was already in high school!! By this time my big brother Neil had a huge problem with resentment to all authority. He got himself into a lot of trouble. We lived in a trailer on ten-acres in the middle of nowhere. Barry really isolated us this time.

He and my mom got me an old 69 Chevy Impala. My car payments were sixty-nine dollars a month, and gas was fifty-cents a gallon. I thought it was a boat!! I didn't get to pick out my own car, but I did get to pay for it. My senior year I had enough credits to only go for four hours. I'd go home change and go to work. It was quite a drive every day, but it kept me out of the house.

I couldn't wait to someday leave that house of horrors! Daniel and I used to work the dinner shift together. I loved that with all we were faced with at home, Daniel had a great sense of humor. He was handsome, and all the girls loved him. Daniel and I had a couple of classes together, so we always went to lunch together. I always had cash, so I always paid for lunch. Ted the breakfast cook started showing up during my shift (when my mom wasn't there) and would sit in my station through my whole shift and talk to me. He always left me a good tip, since I lost money on that table with him sitting there all day. I didn't really care because he was someone who really liked me!

Ted had gotten his divorce and after a short while we started dating after work. He would pick me up at work and take me out. Daniel would stay at his apartment till it was time to go home so we could walk in the door at home together. We could only do this on the weekends, because we still had school. We told our parents it got busy at the restaurant and we had to stay late. They never questioned us.

I'm sure my mom loved us in her own way but, she only showed her affection to Daniel. She always believed everything he would tell her. He was a very special gift from God. Mom ate up his hugs and kisses. He saw past her flaws and flattered her every chance he had, and she ate it up with a spoon while he was winking at us behind her back like "that's how you do it"! He loved her.

Thinking back, he was the only one she showed affection to. I guess it just wasn't there for the rest of us, just not like it was for Daniel. I guess when you're treated different you treat different. Ted took me to my first concert and I still to this day have the T-Shirt! After a while my brothers wanted to go to concerts too, so we all went together. Daniel and I spent every day together, but we never got to enjoy each other outside the house or work. We all would have a great time!

By this time Neil had moved out and gotten married to his high school love, but it didn't last long. None of us were ready for a relationship let alone marriage. We all had physiological problems, some more than others. Barry screwed us all up and mom was never any help. By this time, I knew that Barry meant more to mom than we did.

Once again, we had to move. This time it was close to the school I wanted to graduate from and close to work but. That lasted for only a few months. I never understood why we kept moving so much, but I was glad I got to go and finish my senior year at the school I wanted to go to. After graduation we were moving back to Florida again! By this time, I didn't want to go. I graduated high school and Daniel had to go to summer school and was going to have to do it in Florida in order to get his diploma.

The man I loved was going to be left behind, and I didn't want to go. I told my mom I wanted to stay with Ted in Oklahoma. I was going to be 18 at the end of the summer and I wanted to stay. Barry said if I was still 17, I was going with them. My heart broke. I had to leave Ted behind and I was still a minor and had no choice.

The day came and we packed up our belongings and I closed my bank account. It was 1975 and three to four hundred dollars was a lot of money for someone my age. Every time we stopped for gas or to stretch our legs, I got my siblings and I snacks. Mom brought stuff to make sandwiches. Barry asked where we got the money for the snacks. I told him I had closed my bank account and had some cash. I never should have told him because he took every penny I had, and I never saw it again. He said I needed to help the family with this trip and that was the end of it. He had taken everything he could possibly could away from me, and now all the money I worked so hard for was gone too!

I was broke and broken. The man I loved, my dignity, and my sanity, my free will, it was all gone. Life seemed so bleak to me at the time and I was headed to a deep depression. The few things in life that I enjoyed were taken away from me, and I was sure my life was over. I didn't dare say a word to anyone. I was always shot down anyway and I was the most passive one in the bunch, scared of my own shadow. Barry really did a number on me.

Barry ended up taking my car away from me. He said he needed it more than I did, and I wasn't working yet.

My One True Father

Mom did nothing to stop him. He could do no wrong in her eyes. By the grace of God, I didn't have thoughts of killing myself! That was the last straw. I made up my mind that when I have kids, they were always going to get hugs and kisses. I would always tell them I loved them and protect them no matter what.

One night we got a call. Barry crashed the car while driving drunk. He was fine, but the car was pretty messed up, mostly body damage. He got that fixed and painted and when I got the nerve to ask if I had any money left from the trip, he said that's what paid for the car.

He took so much away from me in my short life! I felt so alone and empty. I wondered what I did wrong in my life to have all this bad luck! I would pray, but I thought that God must have been too busy for me. My siblings started school after that summer and Daniel got a job. I was done. I told my parents I was looking for a job, but I just went to the park every day. I thought my life was over. I prayed a lot and waited for a sign.

I didn't know how praying was going to help me. My belief in God was so slim, because of all the ugliness that was in my life. Little did I know what God had in store for me.

Diane "Broken Arrow" Leeward

My One True Father

Freedom

One day, my brother Neil called my mom and said that he and Ted were coming down for a visit. We had only been gone a month, and I was so excited!!! This news was better than Christmas or any other day of my life! Barry of course said NO! They couldn't stay there. There's no room and he didn't like Ted anyway. I think Barry saw him as a threat. I never told Ted what we had lived through. They came anyway.

The guys got to the house. Mom let Neil sleep on the floor in the living room and said to Ted you can't stay. Mom was so happy to see Neil, but Neil said if Ted can't stay, he couldn't either. Ted took Neil in when we left Oklahoma and gave him a place to live. They both slept on the living room floor. They were best friends and Neil stood by him. It came time for Ted to go back to Oklahoma and Neil decided to stay.

Ted was determined to take me back to Oklahoma. I begged and pleaded and argued with Barry and mom to let me go back with Ted, but they said NO. By this time, I finally stood up to Barry and my mom and told them I was going back to Oklahoma with Ted. Barry reminded me I wasn't quite 18 yet. I was a couple of weeks from my eighteenth birthday. Barry told me if I left, he would call the cops on Ted and have him arrested for taking a minor over the state line.

Mom just stood there. She never said a word and she was never on my side. I don't know where the strength came from because I was and still am very passive. I told Barry (in front of my mom) if you don't let me go, I'll tell the cops what you've been doing to me and my sisters over these years. They looked at me in shock and mom said, "just let her go".

I couldn't believe it! I was free!! (Ted never asked what was said to change my parents mind. At the time he didn't care, and I never spoke of it again. Then I was in shock! Mom let me go without a fight! Just like that! Was she so worried about what would happen to her precious husband and not her flesh and blood! It took me a minute to just not to care and I just wanted to get out of there. As Ted and I started on our journey I felt so guilty leaving my sisters and my brothers behind. It was hard saying goodbye to by siblings especially to my twin. I was so used to seeing him every day all day. Now I didn't know when I would see him next. I prayed and worried about them all for a long time.

Little did I know that after I left, my youngest sisters were Barry's next victims. I didn't know about it until years later when they told me about it. I honestly didn't think Barry would go that far especially with his own daughter.

Ted and I got to Oklahoma and had to stay with his parents until we found our own apartment and got married. He went back to cooking and I went back to waiting tables. Daniel and I kept in touch, we wrote to each other a lot and I missed him so much. This was the first time in my life I was ever away from him and my siblings. School, lunches, work, etc.... we were always together. I never gave a thought to being without him. We were always going to be there for each other. I tried to call often but money was tight and phone calls were expensive. I called home on Thanksgiving and Christmas and a little here and there.

I remember calling Daniel after the New Year with some big news! Guess what? I'm pregnant!!! I think I told him before I told my mom! He was so excited for me and wanted to come see me. He said it was so busy at work right now (it was the busy season) but he would be able to come up by April. I was so happy and couldn't wait to see him. He told his boss and the date was set for April. He couldn't wait to see my belly. I wasn't quite showing yet, but he didn't care.

The time came and Daniel and his friend Sam jumped into Daniels car and headed to Oklahoma. I couldn't wait! I went to bed one night so excited knowing when I woke up the next day my brother would be there. Early that morning the phone rang it was my mom. She was crying and told me Daniel and Sam had been in a car accident. My heart sank. I got a huge lump in my throat and I couldn't talk. Ted took the phone and talked to mom

She went into a little more detail but, she didn't know how badly he was injured. She said she would call me when she knew more. I was numb I had a bad feeling deep in my soul. I waited for my mother to call back. When she did, she said the doctors told her she should get to the hospital. That's all I needed to hear. I told her Ted and I would meet them there.

We drove from Oklahoma to Arlington Texas. I cried the whole way to the point of getting the shakes. Ted tried to keep me calm, think about the baby, and try to stay calm he would say. He was already in love with our baby and all I could focus on was Daniel. I realized that if Daniel needed a kidney or something from me, I was willing to sacrifice my baby to keep him alive.

That was not in God's plan and I didn't know what I was saying. I just knew I was losing a part of myself and my imagination was going in all kinds of awful directions. I was only a few months pregnant and I wasn't connected to that child growing inside me as much as I was connected to Daniel. Ted didn't know what to say. He was shocked to hear what I was saying and so was I. I never knew death before. My brother was the first. It was beyond my understanding. It was the worst day of my life and not having any information on his condition just made it worse.

It took three long hours to get there, and we didn't yet know how he was. I was once again in my own private hell of a different kind. Ted tried his best to keep a positive attitude to keep me calm. We finally got to the hospital. I remember going to the nurse's station and telling the nurse that my brother had been in a car accident and was brought here.

This was forty-three years ago, and they had index cards to look for patients. She pulled his card up, and I'll never forget what I saw. It was Daniels card with EXPIRED written in bright red letters across it. I froze. I thought she was going to tell us his room number and that my parents were there with him waiting for me. Ted called the nurse a few choice names and said that's my wife's twin and my wife is pregnant!

She was so sorry; she hadn't meant for us to see that. She was just going to direct us to the chapel where my mom and Barry were. She said they had a doctor waiting for me just in case I needed him. Ted turned to go to the elevator and I literally couldn't move. I had never felt that before. Ted turned me around and walked me to the elevator. We got in and I couldn't talk or walk, my mind was a blank. People kept getting on and off the elevator and I was ready to jump out of my skin!!

Finally, the doors opened. We found the chapel and I saw my mom. The look on her face will forever be etched in my brain. I lost it and started crying. I blamed myself, and if it weren't for me, he wouldn't have been there. I think I passed out, but there was a doctor there on standby. Mom said he didn't suffer. He never woke up, and he was never in any pain. He's at rest now. We finally left the hospital and found a hotel room after mom made plans to have him transported to Oklahoma.

Barry's parents who once lived in Oklahoma. owned two burial plots there and gave them permission to use one. That night in our hotel room, there were 2 double beds, we took one and my parents took the other. I finally cried myself to sleep.

I woke up in the middle of the night and my brother was looking down on me from the ceiling! I know I wasn't sleeping he was there!

"I'm coming with you," I told him. "I can't live without you! I need you!"

"No, you can't," he replied.

I felt my body float up to the ceiling and I was ready to go, not giving thought to my husband or my child. Daniel was whole and at peace and spoke to me in a very calm tone.

"Ted and your baby girl need you."

I had no idea I was having a girl or boy. He convinced me that he was fine but had to leave me. The good Lord wasn't finished with me yet. I didn't understand that at that time and I didn't care. I was very young, and I just couldn't understand why God would literally take away my other half!

I must tell you I was so mad at God for taking him away from me. This was the worst part of my life Why God? I just didn't understand! I always called him my other half because we came into this world together and that's how we were supposed to stay, together. We were whole. This was supposed to be the best time of my life! I was married to the first man I ever gave my heart to and I was going to be a momma!

The next morning, I woke up, and I thought about the

conversation I had with Daniel. It was real! I was calmer than I was the night before and, for years I never told anyone I spoke to him for fear of people thinking I was crazy. I know in my heart he was there, and I spoke to him. He told me he loved me, and everything would be ok. Even to this day at sixty-two years old I am still comforted by him when I need him.

My entire family from Florida and Texas came to the funeral. It was good to see them all again. I found a way to put aside the feelings I had for my parents. It wasn't easy but, I had no choice. Ted was the only one that I could remember who comforted me. None of us kids ever felt that kind of loss before. That was the first funeral I ever attended, and I never dreamed it would be for Daniel. I cried a lot and I'm sure being pregnant didn't help with the overwhelming feeling of loss mixed with the hormones running through me.

Friends of Daniel's came from Florida. I was so surprised to see them, and one of them was like a brother. Daniel was only in Florida for six or seven months, but he made friends fast. To see them there I knew they were true friends. I'm still in touch with one of them, and he still morns Daniel on the anniversary date of his death as we all do.

Ted was having a hard time making ends meet after that and I couldn't work anymore. He decided he was going to go into the Army. I would go back to Florida and stay with my family until he was out of basic training.

Things with my family was different when I returned. I had been gone a while, I was pregnant, and we had all lost Daniel. We flew by the seat of our pants. Ted and I had no plans whatsoever and a baby on the way! A few weeks before he had to report for duty, we went to the lake with another couple for a picnic and a swim. When we got there, we found a nice spot under a nice tree with a swing rope on it. Well the guys couldn't wait to try it out.

Ted was first and had a blast. Our friend tried it next and they both continued having a great time. Ted was up again and somehow, he slipped and let go of the rope too soon. Little did we know there was broken glass and a lot of other garbage there in the shallow end of the water. Ted slipped and when he came up, he was screaming his head off. I had no idea what happened; it scared me to death.

When he pulled himself out of the water, he was bleeding uncontrollably from his leg. It had one huge gash. We quickly packed up and took him to the nearest hospital. They gave him a tetanus shot and stitched him up. We still had time before he had to report in for duty, so he had a little time to heal. Next thing I knew we were saying goodbye and off to Florida I went. He said we would be back together before the baby was born.

A new life was just what my family needed after losing my brother. My sister Leigh had gotten married and moved to Texas and coincidentally she married the guy who was driving my brothers' car when he was killed. My other sister Ann was still at home, and I got to spend time with her and my two youngest sisters.

We never spoke about Barry and the horrific things he had done to us. It seemed that the nightmare we lived through was behind us. Ted called when he could to check up on me and the baby. He said he was having trouble with his leg. His drill sergeant had made him crawl to the medic when he couldn't walk anymore, and he wouldn't let anyone help him either. I couldn't believe anyone could be so mean! Ted opted out for a medical discharge. He never made it out of boot camp.

It was my nineteenth birthday and I was without my husband or my twin. Daniel, myself and my sister Ann always celebrated our birthdays together because we were only a year and three days apart. I never celebrated my birthday again. I've never been included in my sister's celebration either and that's ok. It wouldn't be the same again anyway. As far as I can remember my name has never been on another birthday cake.

Ted got a medical discharge from the Army a little while after my birthday and sent me a plane ticket back to Oklahoma. We had to stay with his parents because we couldn't afford anywhere else to stay. Now, we're starting over again. We stayed in their spare room and slept on the floor. His little sister wasn't about to let us use her room with a bed even though I was eight months pregnant!

Ted started back to work at his old job and worked double shifts sometimes just so we could afford our own place before the baby came. We did the best we could. We finally got a small furnished two-bedroom apartment. I was always alone, but I had a roof over my head. We never went out and I ate a lot of frozen dinners. Groceries were not in our budget. We didn't even have a phone. Ted ate at work, and I was sleep by the time he got home, so only the necessities were bought.

Mom never taught me how to cook but then she never taught me a lot of things that a mother should have taught her daughter. Getting out of that house was my goal. Mother daughter moments were something that weren't going to happen and that was just fine with me. I always had to clean and to do laundry, dishes, etc. when I was at home so, in my new home it was always a clean home. I was so OCD at my parents' home, because if it wasn't done right, I had to do it again.

It was now getting close to my due date, and I got a letter from my mom. She was going to send my sister Ann to help me for a short time before and after the baby was born. I was so excited! We put her in our spare room. We didn't have a crib yet. Right before the baby was born Ted came home with a crib that someone set out for the garbage. Ann and I cleaned it up and painted it. We had a small bassinet that Ted's sister gave us.

The morning came soon after Ann got there. I went into labor. Ted wasn't home yet and I screamed to my sister to go to a neighbor's house to call Ted at work. To my surprise not one neighbor opened their door to her. Maybe because she sounded like a crazy person. LOL!! Finally, Ted got home, and he got us to the hospital in one piece. There's never a cop around when you need one, and I'm thankful we got there safe.

Ted had just worked a double shift and was extremely tired. I was so afraid of going into my hospital room, because I could hear other women going into labor. They sounded like they were all being tortured. I must say I didn't want to sound that way. I got settled in and was all hooked up to the monitors and all that was left was to have patience. This was my first time in a hospital, and I was scared to death.

Ted sat in a chair next to me throughout the labor and never heard me scream during contractions. The pain was like I had never experienced in my life! Thank God for my sister. She was there for me when Ted couldn't be. He literally slept through it. I squeezed Ann's hand so hard a couple of times, I thought I broke it and she did too! The nurse asked if I wanted something for the pain, and that I didn't have to go through all that. I noticed the girl in the bed next to me, and she was so doped up that she didn't even know where she was. I told her no thank you.

I knew at that moment I had to ask God to help me. For the first time since my brother died, I asked God for help. God was there for me the whole time. I was just so full of heartache for the last year of my life. I didn't ask God for anything. I didn't even talk to him. If you know me now, you know I talk to God every day all day.

Next thing I remember the doctor was asking me if we were ready to meet our baby. The doctor had to use forceps for delivery. My baby girl was here! I was concerned about the red marks on her face and her head was shaped odd. The doctor said she would be ok in a few hours. I couldn't wait to call my mom and tell her she was a grandmother. She was already a grandmother from my oldest brother, but none of us got to spend much time with her.

Our baby was 7lbs 5oz. and 21 inches long. She was beautiful! In an instant I thought about Daniel, and I prayed to God that he could see her. God took my brother, but he gave me this beautiful child to fill the void in my heart. I felt like she's the only thing in my life I've ever done right. I've been so used to being told how stupid I was, that I thought my life was just so insignificant. God changed that for me. Now I have this perfect little person who depends on me and needs me. I think my daughter's birth brought me back to God. God did have a plan for me.

I will never understand how mom could ever let anyone hurt any of her babies. The love I feel for this baby changed my life! We didn't have much, but I always told her I would always love and protect her. We named her Dawn. I used to pray that God was letting Daniel watch over her throughout her life and help me keep her safe. Now I know what Daniel was trying to tell me. "SHE needs me". She's been my baby girl ever since.

Shortly after we took Dawn home, I got a letter from my mom. Her coworkers got together and bought her a plane ticket to come see me and her new granddaughter. I've never seen my mom with that kind of love in her eyes. Mom needed this new life in her life too. She called Dawn" the apple of her eye". I was so excited to see my mom. She gave me advice on what to do. I had no idea what I was doing in my life let alone how to take care of a baby. Sure, I could change a diaper and feed a baby, but the rest was a responsibility I took seriously.

Barry took away any part of my self-esteem and confidence that I might have had and reduced me to being afraid of my own shadow. I had to take care of this precious gift from God, and I wasn't going to let her down. I was going to be a different mother to my daughter than what my mother was to me. Come hell or high water! Ted was a bit of a stoner and I told him if he keeps it away from Dawn I didn't care. I had no control over him, and he worked hard. He didn't drink, so that was his relaxation.

A few months later Ted came home from work and told me that they needed a hostess a few hours a night, a couple of nights a week at the restaurant if I was interested. He said he would be home with the baby while I was working. I jumped at the chance, because I was ready to step out into the world again. The first night all I thought about was my baby, but I knew her dad was with her.

Diane "Broken Arrow" Leeward

My One True Father

More Changes

It was New Year's Eve and my first time away from my baby. They closed after the dinner shift, so I got home early. When I got home and opened the door, our apartment was full of people I didn't know. They were all drinking and smoking weed and that was the first meltdown I ever had. I looked for my baby then kicked everyone out. I was so mad at Ted!

Shortly after that we saved up and moved to Florida. I needed to be near my family. I was not so surprised to hear that Barry left mom for a younger woman. No one kept me in the loop of what was going on at home. Funny thing mom followed him around town until she caught him and played the victim card. I thought why didn't you show a little concern for us when we were little?

I felt like karma just bit her! That's what betrayal taste like. She always knew what he was doing to us but never came to our rescue. One day I asked her why she did nothing and she told me, "how can I take care of all you kids by myself?" Yet she always told people she worked two jobs to take care of us. I guess she forgot about all the husbands who helped with a paycheck. I asked why not a hug or a kiss, it would have helped. Mom just didn't have that motherly touch. Barry was her focus not her kids. Then I remembered Barry once told me if I told anyone what he did no one would believe me, and if they did all of us kids would go into foster care. We would never see each other again. I was young and I believed him. God does answer prayers and he's out of our lives.

Barry ended up marrying the woman he had an affair with and had two more kids with her, a boy and a girl. The wife ended up leaving him for her preacher. I don't know if he molested his other daughter or not! Barry's son stayed behind to take care of him, not knowing what he had done to his sister or the rest of us.

Mom in the meantime married one of Barry's best friends. I guess that was her way of sticking it to him. My two youngest sisters didn't like him and made his life hell. He had never been married before and tried to boss them around a lot. They weren't having it. After living through Barry, they weren't going to let another man impose himself on them again in any way shape or form.

Mom would send my youngest sister to her father (Barry) when she could no longer control her. She knew what he would do to her, so my youngest sister left and moved in with her childhood friend. She was only fourteen or fifteen. I felt so bad for my sisters, but mom finally got rid of husband number four.

The girls are fine now, physically anyway. Deep down we're all broken inside. We each have our own issues with our mom, but we all act like our mom was the best mom ever! It's an act we all do to be good daughters. It gets us through the day and mom's ego is intact. We've tried to put our past lives behind us and look forward to a bright future. To this day we all act like we had perfect lives. When we tell our children our childhood stories, we only pick out the good parts.

Ted got a job in a nearby restaurant. We found a two-bedroom duplex, and I got a waitress job close by. Dawn was now about a year old. Ted and I were stressed out with all the moving, and new jobs. It took its toll on us. I never told Ted about my childhood. I didn't want him to look at me with pity in his eyes. I was already broken, and I didn't want to be pitied by him. He probably would have understood, but I just couldn't relive it again. I kept making excuses as to why I didn't want to make love to him. When we did, I couldn't wait till it was over. God help me I loved him I just didn't think he would like that I didn't tell him before then.

I was just not equipped to handle this kind of emotional situation. I know he would've understood, but my shame was overwhelming. I just couldn't. It was my dirty secret, and I just lived with it. Ted started showing up in the parking lot at my job. He wanted to know who the customer was I was talking to. He started asking about the odometer in the car. He was asking all kind of strange questions. What did I know about that? What's wrong with you? Why are you acting like that?

Back then we would get these hang-up calls or wrong number calls and hang up. Ted thought I had a secret boyfriend! I was so shocked! Are you kidding me? He started calling me a couple of days a week from work and say he was working a double shift and would be home in the morning. I had no reason to doubt him. Then one day he says, "look I think we need a break or we're not going to make it." I stood in disbelief and said, "ok." If that's how he felt maybe a few days apart would help our relationship. I called mom to see if Dawn and I could stay with her for a little while.

I told her Ted and I were having some problems and needed a little time apart. She said we could. There was no "man" in the house, so I felt safe. We took some stuff to moms, but we forgot Dawns favorite doll, so we went back for it. Ted wasn't expecting to see me and when we got there, he was moving his girlfriend in!!!

My One True Father

When I saw this the devastation set in. He totally blindsided me! He was cheating on me, and that's why he was accusing me and acting so jealous. Was I that ignorant? I felt every name my stepfather called me was true! I totally trusted Ted, I loved him. I'm done with him! I took my daughter and left. I told mom what happened, and she let us stay until I could get my own place.

I worked nights, so I wouldn't have to put Dawn in daycare. Mom took care of her at night, and she was asleep by the time I got home. It was a perfect set up. Mom loved having Dawn, and I didn't have to worry about her. Mom finally stepped up for me. Without a man in the house I had her attention.

One night one of my co-workers asked me to go out with them for a drink. "Just one drink," they said. I was twenty-one years old and had never drank before. The smell of beer made me nauseated. Barry had that smell on his breath every time he jumped into my bed. Until this day I've never had a beer and the smell of it still makes me gag.

My friend said she would get me a sweet fruit drink that I would like. I called my mom before she went to bed and asked if she was ok with it. She was. And added "have a good time." Dawn would be sleeping so no problem. There were a lot of people, music, dancing, and drinking. I didn't know how to act! This was all new to me. It was my first time in a bar, and I was so scared.

One of my other co-workers had a brother she introduced to me. He was cute. "Why was he talking to me," I thought. Well, I was having a great time and now I had a social life! It was the disco days and I learned to dance. I finally had enough money for an apartment, but I needed a roommate. A co-worker knew someone who needed a place to stay so we agreed to try it out. She was great and became a good friend. Life was good.

One night at work a few cops came in and I waited on them. They could see the innocence in me and asked if I ever went out and where. It was a date. My friend and I met them there one night and we all had a lot of fun. I went home after a few hours. I had a baby at home. This one guy kept coming in to see me at work and we started dating. His name was Dick. He was a bit of a player. It didn't work out for long, but we did have a good time. I walked into our favorite bar one night and found another girl on his lap. I really had trust issues but, to save myself any more heartache it's me or nothing.

I thought men were nothing but pigs! One day I asked my mom about my real father. She said he abandoned us a long time ago and didn't want anything to do with us. I knew his name and the area he lived, so I called information and got an address for him. It was not like having the internet that we have today. You must do some leg work. I sent a letter to him, and low and behold, I got an answer back!! We became pen pals.

I told my sister Ann and he wanted to meet us. Mom was sorry she told me anything about him. Ann and I decided to go meet him. He was driving a big rig at the time and was going to be near Orlando. We talked for a little while, but we were strangers. Ann and Daniel Sr. seemed to get along. I told him about my Daniel in a letter. He was very sad about that. Neil wanted nothing to do with him. Whatever mom told him about our father didn't set well with him. God only knows what mom told him.

I was now curious about my father. I wasn't really feeling the love like Ann was. I started to trust my instincts, and I let him go. There were too many unanswered questions, and mom wasn't telling the truth. Ann kept in touch with him over the years and that's fine. I rarely heard from him since then. I put yet another father behind me.

I started meeting a lot of people by now and I was working mornings by this time. Dawn had to go into daycare. The morning crowd at my job were a whole different kind of people. I like it though. I met nice people, and of course not so nice people. By this time, I was finally divorced, and Ted went back to Oklahoma. He would send me seventy-five dollars every now and then for Dawn. I was happy to have her no matter what.

Almost every summer Ted would send a plane ticket for her and she would spend the summer with him. I really struggled with that, because I was so scared, he wouldn't send her back.

My One True Father

Nothing Again

I met a guy named Fred. He came in everyday for coffee, and he started to take a real interest in me. I wanted nothing to do with him. One day I snuck out the back door just to avoid him and was afraid he would follow me. He was seventeen years older than me, and I was just not interested. He was persistent and backed off a little when he realized he was scaring me.

After a while I agreed to go to dinner with him. Fred was a perfect gentleman and didn't try anything funny. We became an item after a few weeks. I never met anyone like him before. He was very interesting and had a lot of stories. He had the most beautiful blue eyes I had ever seen. He told me he was divorced and had a daughter a year older than Dawn and two step-kids.

Fred was a pilot once upon a time. He was also a cop in Ft. Lauderdale. He had a lot of stories. My birthday was coming up and he wanted to take me to the Bahamas for the weekend and I said yes. I was so excited! I had never been anywhere before! I didn't know my roommate had a surprise party planned for me. She got very upset when I told her I wasn't going to be home. She was so upset she moved out the next month. I didn't know about the party.

She thought Fred had too much of an influence over me. She and I had a lot of fun together.

Soon enough, Fred moved in with Dawn and me. He bought me new furniture to replace the recycled stuff that came with the apartment. We went to the Bahamas for a day in a small Queen Air that he piloted. We saw a plane under the water! We landed on a small island and had lunch in a small run-down restaurant that looked shabby. I thought to myself "this is the Bahamas"? There was someone there Fred needed to meet with, so he asked me to stay put until he came back.

We finished lunch and got the hell out of there. I had a bad feeling about the whole thing and was glad we left. On the way home I was shaken but too afraid to ask any questions. Dawn sat in the co-pilot seat with Fred. The next thing I know he came walking to the back to talk to me. "who's flying the plane," I asked shocked.

"Dawn," he replied.

It was on automatic pilot! She really got a kick out of that. We got back home, and I was so relieved. I never went back. We went on the road again. He had a 32-foot Trojan that he said was his. "What did I get myself into," I thought, "Who was this guy?" He owned a small trophy store across the street from where I worked. Somehow, he always explained things away. One of his best friends was a local cop that I had known for years. He always told me that Fred was a good guy and he really loved me. I took a leap of faith and believed him.

Fred started bringing his little girl over on the weekends, and she and Dawn got along well. We started doing a lot of family things together. I thought now I have my own family. He finally bought a house and his step-kids started coming over. We had birthday parties, Easter Sunday brunches, Disney trips. I felt like I had it all!

I still had my old car, and Fred started out in his Jeep. He later came home in a Cadillac and later a corvette. He had a jeep when I met him. Like I said earlier he always explained it away. He said his family had money, and it was no big deal.

His ex-wife, Karen, got the house and a new car. She was good at letting us keep the kids, because she worked a lot. I didn't Mind. She was always getting in touch with him through his beeper. Beepers were all the craze in those days. I wanted to know what all that was all about.

She was a dispatcher at the police station where he once worked, and always kept him informed of what was going on there. I was wondering why he knew so many cops that were my customers. It was because he also taught self-defense in the police academy. Finally, he told me that the reason he wasn't a cop any more was he was arrested on drug charges. He said he was working undercover with the feds. He was an ex-pilot and they needed his skills. Well I bought it, but the police didn't.

What didn't that man do? I was mesmerized by him. He was like 007! I found him very exciting, but at the same time I knew I was always being lied to. He had an answer for everything and as naïve as I was, I believed him. I was never prepared for life. I had no idea what I was doing! He told me that this thing with the drug charges was going to be dropped. Everything was going to be fine. Don't worry. So again, I trusted him. I'll never learn. He played on my passive nature.

I wasn't the type who screamed and yelled. I just went with the flow. In my mind if you wanted to get along just go with the flow and most of the time I did and was fine. I wanted to belong somewhere and to someone who loved me.

I didn't want to make the mistake of keeping it a secret. Full disclosure was the best thing I could do. I couldn't deal with jealousy. I told Fred about my childhood and what I went through as a child through my teen years. I needed Fred to understand, and he did. He never in all the years we were together yelled at me or showed any signs of jealousy. I was thankful for that.

People could be very cruel sometimes. Fred and I had seventeen years between us. Fred was 38 when I met him, and I was 23. People would assume that either I was a gold digger, or he was my sugar daddy and was having a mid-life crisis. We used to get hate mail and awful looks in public.

One night for Valentine's Day he took me to a nice place for dinner. It was so fancy. No one had ever taken me anywhere like that before. I always got carded and that was embarrassing. That night I wore a black spaghetti strap dress and heals. I'll never forget, because I've never had a dress like that before. Fred went to the men's room during our meal, and I noticed a man at the next table with a group of guys staring at me. Next thing I know he's coming my way, but I pretended I didn't notice him.

"You're a beautiful young lady," he said. I responded with thank you. What he said next floored me. "How much," he asked. I was naïve and responded with, "how much what?" His reply was, "You know, how much for a date." I was shocked. He thought I was a hooker! I didn't know what to say. Thank God Fred came back to the table, and the guy left.

Fred asked me what the guy wanted, and It was my turn to lie. I said he wanted to know the time. Oh my God he thought I was a hooker! I couldn't stop saying that in my head. I thought to myself "is that what I look like dressed up like this with Fred?" We never did that again. I told Fred I'm not that fancy person. I appreciated what he did.

The next day I told him what really happened. He got very angry that I lied to him, but I knew he would have punched the guy's lights out. Time passed and Fred finally asked me to marry him and I agreed to. Let's do this! We didn't have a wedding just a couple of close friends and a justice of the peace.

About a week before we got married Fred had some bad news. Karen called and told him that there was a problem with their divorce, and we had to wait. I was so upset. I thought she was trying to ruin our plans. I decided to ask her, so I spoke in a calm voice, "are you was the reason we had to wait?" She calmly said to me, "well, WE have to be divorced first before he can marry you."

"What? You're not divorced?"

"No," she replied, "I'm sorry he did this to you, but think about what you're doing."

Fred wasn't home yet but was expected to be soon. When he walked in the door and saw me crying, I asked, "what was the glitch that was keeping us from getting married?"

He said some lie about the paperwork got misplaced and they had to go through the process again. I looked at him and said, "AGAIN!" I took a deep breath and said to him, "I spoke to Karen!" I literally saw the blood drain from his face. I proceeded to tell him what she told me.

"You never filed for a divorce! Don't lie to me on this!" After I had him backed into a corner, he told me the truth. I was so mad. I told him I wasn't going to marry him, and I never wanted to see him again. Now I know why he put everything in my name and talked me into changing my name before we got married. Yes, I did that. I don't even remember why I did that!

After I cooled down, I called Karen and apologized to her. I had no idea. He was afraid she would take everything that we had in their divorce settlement. How slick can anyone be? She was very gracious and said, "I know how Fred is and it's no big deal, we've been over for a long time." Turns out, Karen didn't want Fred any more than he wanted her. She never gave us a problem and we always got his daughter on the weekends. Fred never paid child support. I didn't get that, but it was none of my business. That was my first year with Fred, and after I got over his deception, I married him.

I was so in love. We finally got into a good spot in our lives, and so we called his mother who lived in N.J. and told her the good news. I had spoken to her a few times on the phone but never met her. She seemed nice, but she was like a social butterfly up there. She was the founder of Future homemakers of America back in her day. She had been on the cover of seventeen magazines back in 1959. Fred told me that they went to Europe every summer, and that his father's family owned a steamship company.

His dad passed when Fred was in the service and his mother was ashamed of him after he got arrested. Fred also had an older sister who was a lot like his mother and had little to do with him either.

After two years we found out we were pregnant. Fred was over the moon. He had another daughter from his first marriage. We never met until much later when she was older. He was somewhat of a stranger to her. Her name was Lynn and her mother's name were Debbie. Debbie was always in touch with Fred's mother because of Lynn. She was a pretty little blond haired blue-eyed little beauty.

Fred's whole family was blue eyed except for Beth, she has beautiful brown eyes. We never really had a lot to do with them. Debbie was very jealous of me because when she and Fred were married, he was having an affair with

Karen. Debbie was remarried but would have left her husband for Fred if she thought she had a chance with him. I was so young she knew she didn't stand a chance.

One day Fred got a call from his attorney, and he had to go meet with him. I thought all this business was over. Turns out the plane, boat, belonged to drug smugglers. The money he was bringing home wasn't from making trophies. I had to sign over the corvette to the attorney. This time things got real. Fred was going to jail. He had been out on appeal and never told me. By then I was ready to give birth, and he would be able to see his son before he left. I gave birth in September. Fred had to leave on a ten-year sentence in December. I didn't know what to do.

We had been renting a room to one of our friends and brought in some rent money. We had a couple of months to figure things out. We were going to lose the house.

I went back to work. I came home from work sick and Fred was there. I thought he was at work. I walked into our bedroom and he was hard at work on one of my co-workers! Why? What was I doing wrong this time? I was done. This time it was like getting hit with a 2x4 and someone saying, "you get it now?"

Oh, he tried to talk himself out of that one but, this time I was done. He was leaving, and I had no future, and no husband.

NOTHING! AGAIN!

The day came when he had to surrender himself to the sheriffs and just like that he was gone. Fred had a K-9 dog that no one could get close to. I didn't know what to do with him. I finally gave him to a security business. The small town that we lived in everyone knew my business, and I couldn't go anywhere without people looking at me and talking behind my back.

My mother told me to put my things in storage and move in with her for a little while. I sold my jeep and some guns to a couple of cops who knew what Fred had. They said they would do me a favor and take them off my hands. They gave me nothing for them, but I had no other choice. Once again, I was taken advantage of by a couple of men who used me to get what they wanted. I truly believed in them and thought they were my friends. My house reverted to its owner. Fred had bought me a van for all the kids before all this mess happened. He had paid cash for it so at least I had that.

. One day Ted called to see if he could have our daughter for the holidays. Of course, I said, now? Behind my back my mother had been talking to my ex-husband and telling him all my troubles. I've lost everything. The man I loved and hated at the same time was gone too. All I had was my kids. I lost my job because I couldn't face anyone anymore. The looks and whispers were too much.

Ted said you have got to know I still love you, and I never stopped. He was so sorry for everything and his excuse for cheating on me was "I was young and stupid". He invited me and the kids to Oklahoma to spend the holidays with him with the option to come back if it didn't work out. What did I have to lose?

A part of me will always belong to Ted. He was my real first love and the father of my daughter. Ted was good to us, and it felt good to hold my head up somewhere where no one knew me. I guess now I was using him to get away from my troubles, and he was ok with that. Ted just wanted another chance and said he would raise Fred Jr. as his own. I just wanted a new life, and this was it. My emotions were running rampant and Ted said, "I promise things will be different". We spent the holidays in Oklahoma. We flew back to Florida after the holidays and cleaned out my storage unit and used a U-Haul truck to go back to Oklahoma. We sold some of the things we couldn't take and had enough money for the down payment on a small house. I knew there was some love for him left in my heart. Ted was very patient with me.

In the meantime, Fred was calling my mother looking for me, but she wouldn't tell him where I went. They moved him around a lot because he was an ex-cop. I finally told her to tell him where I was after all I had his son. Mom finally gave him my phone number and of course he told me of his undying love for Jr. and me. I told him I filed for divorce, and that I was starting over in Oklahoma with Dawn's father.

That's right I married my first husband again! To my surprise he said good, and that he just wanted me to be happy. He also said that once he got out, he would like to have a relationship with his son. I told Ted about the call and he was ok with it. He asked me how many years Fred had. It was ten but could be three with good behavior.

Fred gave his mother my phone number. She called. She was concerned about the grandson she had never met. She also had to tell me how her son was doing. She saw him as a disgrace to the family, and really wanted nothing to do with him. She did feel sorry for him because he lost everything. I felt bad so I started sending her pictures of her grandson. I didn't know, but she started to send them to Fred. He wrote to me and told me that his mother was sending him the pictures.

The day the first letter came in the mail my heart

skipped a beat. I didn't know where he got my address. I told his mother not to give it to him, but he pleaded with her so much that she gave in to him. He was a very good manipulator. I didn't know what to do. I felt bad for him, but he wasn't my problem anymore. He would tell me how much he missed me and Jr., and how much he still loved me. He even said he found God. Funny how NOW you find God. He started sending me scriptures and stories and of course I fell for it. He rekindled the love I knew I still had because it was never settled. I didn't give myself time! Now I had to deal with this.

I was a stay at home mom that year. I had a neighbor that I hung out with, and I started to tell her about my dilemma. I would sit and talk to her all the time. I made so many bad decisions in my life, and I didn't know how to get off the ride. I couldn't talk to my mother because, let's face it I couldn't trust her. Every time I visited her, I started smoking pot, it was the only way I could deal with her. I never told Ted I smoked pot, because I didn't want to tempt him. One of us needed to be sober.

The letters stopped for a while and later found out Fred had been moved to another facility. Ted my current husband could tell something was wrong. When he asked, I just told him I was bored, and I didn't know anyone except our neighbor. I didn't like going out in public. I was still ashamed of what happened back in Florida.

Time passed and Ted said it was time to put Jr. in daycare so I could get a job. That's when I told him about Fred and the letters. I never got closure. I found myself still in love with both. There was no way this wasn't going to hurt him, and I was just so sorry. I couldn't explain what I didn't understand myself. Please God help me! Ted called my mom and told her what was going on. She said I need to stop acting crazy and stay with him. I felt that she wanted Ted out of my life so we could have to stay with her for a while.

I understood how upset Ted was. He started drinking and getting stoned more often. We didn't talk for days. One night he got so wasted I thought he was going to hit me. I ran with my kids to the neighbor's house for a while. I knew this fear oh so well. I thought to myself there's no going back from this. He wasn't going to trust me anymore, and now I was now afraid of him.

He would punish me by taking my keys when he went to work. He never left money in case I needed it. One day his fears came true, I told him I was leaving him and taking the kids. There was nothing else to do. I stopped talking to my mom while all this was going on. I was already messed up and she was never any help to me anyway. I made up my mind and I was leaving.

Diane "Broken Arrow" Leeward

God's Help

Fred was over the moon to say the least. He was in a facility in Texas. I packed up my van and the kids and only took what I needed. I left everything I ever owned. I had a port-a-crib for Jr. and cloths for the kids and a few toys. Dawn was about seven-years old currently and Jr. was a year. Ted gave me two hundred dollars and said goodbye and good luck.

I know I hurt him very much and there was nothing he could do about it. He had to know the pain he put me through once upon a time. This was something we didn't see coming. I didn't know where I was going, or what I was doing. I couldn't find my way out of a paper bag. I never felt so alone, and now I was dragging my babies with me. Please God help me! Little did I know, He heard me, and took care of us. Dawn was such a life saver. She helped me with Jr. while I was driving. She would change his diaper and give him a bottle while I drove. She would then come back to the front and sit with me and we would sing along to some cassettes that we liked. It made the time pass.

I thought to myself oh my God I've messed up my life and now my kids! Dawn was such a trooper. I couldn't have done it without her. She was my right arm and my heart.

She looked up to me, and I couldn't let her down. I found a rundown hotel outside of the prison, and we stayed there. I was ready for a good night's sleep and so were the kids. I had enough money for the room for two nights and something for the kids to eat.

There was enough left for a simple meal, milk and diapers for Jr. and gas money. I didn't eat. I wanted to make sure the kids had enough. The next day was visiting day, Saturday. I had never been so scared in my life. We drove through these big gates. The jail looked like a big palace on a hill and a few buildings around it. They were called Camps. A camp was where the less dangerous prisoners were kept, and that's where Fred was.

After all the bags were checked we finally got to go in and see Fred. Dawn ran to him, and still called him daddy. Jr. didn't know him, but he got used to him in a very short time. They had a chapel at the facility, and we went there the next day. Fred introduced me to a couple of his buddies and their families. Everyone was very nice. The talked about how they thought Fred was making us up. Our story was a bit unusual.

Fred did a lot of praying; I never saw this side of him before. I was impressed. Fred was worried, because he had no idea what we had ahead of us. He was limited in what he could do to help us. That's when God took over.

After we left, I found myself wondering, what do I do next. What direction would I take literally? My reasoning was I had come in from the right, so I took a left! I found myself eighty-five miles away from my grandmother's house! I realized where I was! Thank you, God, He had brought me to the one person I needed the most.

As I pulled up to her house my heart was pounding with excitement. I was overwhelmed with joy. We were safe! When we pulled up, Grandma was sitting on her front porch. She didn't know who the van belonged to, but when she saw me, she ran to me with open arms. My aunt still lived next door. My other aunt from down the street came over to see who was at grandma's house. They all hugged me and were surprised to see me. They were curious as to why it was only me and the kids.

I got caught up on things. I was surprised to find out my grandmother married my Aunt's father-in-law. I've known him my entire life. He was already like a grandfather to me, and he was my cousin's grandfather. I was very happy to know he married my grandma. They were both alone for a very long time.

We all sat on the front porch and as I told my aunts my story, they translated it to my grandma. She cried with me and held me. She said me and they kids could stay if we needed to. My cousin who lived across the street extended the same invitation. God sure knew what he was doing when he sent me to my grandmother's. I needed her so much.

Later that night one of my aunts called my mom to let her know I was there. Mom would call to check in on me. Time passed and my grandma's house was finally updated. One of my aunts put a phone in her house. Mom started calling me regularly. She often asked me to come home and she would take care of us. She made us visiting the jail sound like a bad thing. She was relentless, but I kept refusing her offer. Eventually I asked her to stop calling. She didn't like Fred and her calls caused a lot of grief.

My grandmother taught me how to forgive, and that had been the biggest challenge of my life at that time. I felt like I was a little girl again, back in time with my grandma. The smell of fresh tortillas in the morning with coffee and eggs. She said I was too skinny and needed to gain some weight. She didn't want Fred to think she wasn't taking care of me. She had no idea what a blessing she was to me and my kids. I told her every day how much I loved her and thanked God for her. Her hugs were one of the most precious things I remember about her. She cried with me, held me, and prayed with me every day I was there.

My One True Father

The small town hadn't changed much since I was a kid. My cousins still lived there, and it felt like home again. It was our favorite vacation spot. They loved Barry here. He was funny and the token funny gringo. They didn't know him like we did, and we didn't dare say anything to anyone. I talked to Fred's mother and told her where I was. I wanted her to tell him so he wouldn't worry. She started sending me a hundred dollars a month, so I would have money to go see Fred on the weekends.

I couldn't take food inside, I had to buy things from the vending machines. After the weekends I went back to grandmas. She was so worried about me every time I left, and so happy to see me back. I did my best to help her around the house, and if I had money left, I would buy groceries. Sometimes I would take grandma to another town thirty-five miles away to get her monthly groceries. While we were out, I would take her out to lunch. That was a big deal to her. She tried to give me money one time for taking her to the store and I refused. Apparently, anyone who took her for groceries also charged her for gas. I was so upset about that!

Grandma's house was the hangout place to go first thing in the morning. She would make everyone breakfast and coffee, but no one ever helped her with the cost. She and I used to sit on the front porch and talk a lot. Grandma sat and listened and cried with me. She would tell me not to be so hard on my mother. She felt my mom loved me. Grandma had no idea what mom made us live through.

The love and compassion grandma showed me was what I wished my mother gave me. She would trust me with her secrets and always made me promise not to tell anyone. Everyone always told her what to do and not to do. She had come to really resent it but was too afraid to speak up for herself. I now know where I got my passiveness from. Grandma, lived on a tight budget, but my Aunt May always helped her, and I tried to do the same when I could. I love her so much.

One day I was at my cousin's house with the kids. My cousin wasn't there but had gone to her parent's house which was next door to grandma's. Her uncle was there visiting and wanted to see him. Well my cousin was a bit of a busy body, town gossip. What she heard everyone talking about changed my life forever.

My cousin comes back home. As soon as she came in, she tells me she must tell me something that I was not going to believe.

"I have to tell you something that you're not going to believe!"

"Ok what is it?"

"Have you ever met my uncle Diego?"

"I don't think," I replied. I didn't know all her father's siblings.

"He knows you!"

"Why?"

"I heard him tell my mom and dad that you were his daughter, and he had come to meet you."

"WHAT," I was floored.

I called my mother right away and asked who he was and why would he say such a thing? I've never met him. He didn't live there. I was full of questions. She emphatically denied everything that I asked her and wanted me to come home. Now I knew why she wanted me home so much. Her dirty little secret was out! I was so upset and didn't know what to do or who to believe. Mom wasn't giving up any information. I just quit taking her phone calls.

My father called me at my cousin's house. I was trying to understand what I just learned. I wanted to know if he could come over and talk to me. He said he would and that I must have a lot of questions and that he would try his best to answer them. He came over and introduced himself and proceeded to tell me his and my mother's history.

They had known each other since they were kids. They all grew up together! My uncle had a major crush on my mother, but my father won her over. My uncle ended up marrying my aunt (mom's sister, dad's brother). Two brothers hooked up with two sisters. I just can't make this stuff up! Growing up in this small town. Everyone knew, but never said a word to me. My grandparents were my real blood grandparents! My grandmother was so upset that she couldn't tell me. It wasn't her secret to tell and she was trying to be loyal to her daughter. I must respect that, and my mother never thought I would find out.

Dad's conscious finally got the best of him, I guess. I like to think that this was a part of God's plan for me. What else could it be? That same year I was told that my older brother Neil was also my father's son. Neil had been told the truth, because he and our half-sister had started dating. After Neil found out he started to treat our father like he was entitled to my dad's life because he was his son.

He started demanding things, so my mom recanted her story. My dad didn't have him arrested. After that my brother changed his last name to my mother's maiden name. He lost his identity and mom refused to tell him the truth.

My One True Father

My poor brother is so screwed up, and Mom says the full moon is to blame. To this day my brother barely talks to my mother. He loves her, but he's hurting. He can't forget the way we grew up. I know the feeling.

I stopped talking to my mother for almost a year. I had a daddy who would've loved my twin brother and I, but we didn't have a say in it. Mom robbed me and my brothers of the father we always wanted and deserved to have. Her selfish choices cost us a lot. Mom's reputation meant more to her than protecting her kids.

Talk about God stepping in, I never would've found my father if I hadn't taken that leap of faith. I put my life in God's hands, and he gave me my father. I prayed a lot, but I still didn't understand the depth of what God had in mind for me. It was God's plan in my life. I didn't know why my life took this turn, but it did.

I asked my father why he didn't say anything to me until now? He told me that mom was married, and she begged him not to say a word. She said her husband would take good care of us, so they went on their own way with their own lives never to tell anyone that he was my father. It was a small town; everyone knew everything about everyone. A lifetime passed. He told me that when Daniel died a part of him died too. He suffered in silence.

His wife told me she didn't know why he went into such a deep depression. At the time she didn't know what happened to make him feel that way. It took a long time, before he finally told her about us. My uncle (his brother) always kept my dad informed about us. That's how he knew so much about me. When I showed up in town again, my uncle told him it was time I knew who he was, and that I might need him. In other words, "man up." I asked dad about doing a DNA test and he said there was no need, he knew I was his.

I finally saved enough money to rent a small apartment for me and the kids. It was in a town near the prison. I didn't have to travel so much with the kids. It was a two-bedroom, 1 bath, furnished, with electric included for three-hundred-fifty dollars a month. I had to find a job. I never asked anyone for money, and no one offered me help. I'm sure mom probably never told my siblings the truth about what I was going through. Mom's biggest secret was out, and I'm sure she wasn't going to tell a soul.

I was so thankful to God for sending me to this place. All the neighbors were so nice, loving and offered help anytime I needed. All the neighborhood kids walked to school together. A few moms who didn't work walked with the kids too. I felt very comfortable letting my little girl go with them every morning. They would bring her home with them every afternoon. I worked, and they would keep her until I got home.

My son was just a year old or so, and I found a YMCA to take him. I was very fortunate to get a spot for him. I had to go and apply for food stamps and daycare. When you are at that point in your life and you must feed your kids; you do what you must. I had all I needed. Thank you, God, I got a job working in the school cafeteria, so I could have the weekends off with my kids and go to see Fred. The weekends were the only visiting days.

I can't believe what God has brought me through. It was a perfect set up. My dad drove a semi-truck and came through our town once a week and he always stopped by to see me and the kids. I loved him. He was the Dad I always wanted, and God answered my prayers. He would bring the kids toys and his wife would send blankets along with other things. We had the bare minimum. She was very kind to us. I felt very fortunate that she accepted us at all.

One day dad and his wife invited me and the kids to go meet my half-sister. Boy I was flying blind. I didn't know what I was doing, but we got to his home for the weekend. He took us all out and showed us a good time. My kids loved it. My sister didn't like me very much. I instantly felt the resentment. She was an only child and had everything she ever wanted. Now she had to share her daddy. I suppose I don't blame her. She was just as blindsided as I was. She is a couple of years younger than me and had a son and a daughter.

I never knew I had another family and I was so confused on how I was supposed to feel or act. Now I know whose face was looking back at me every time I investigated a mirror; it was my dad's. I had prayed so long for answers, but mom wasn't giving me any. We had a nice time despite the awkwardness. Dad really tried hard. I guess he was trying to make up for lost time; he also felt so guilty.

I finally got a phone because my job as A cafeteria worker was as needed. It kept sending me to different schools in the city. I was on call until I got a permanent school to work at. I finally did, and I got along with all my co-workers but one. The head cook had the hots for a very good-looking janitor. If he looked my way and smiled, she went off! They were both married but not to each other. She saw me as a threat. I told her I didn't want him or anyone else. I had Fred and that's all I wanted. I told the kitchen manager my situation. Thank God she was a Christian woman and sympathized with my situation and got her off my back!

She knew her cook was wrong to be acting like that

with a married man, and she had a talk with her. Our first summer there one of my youngest sisters came out to visit with her baby girl. I was so happy to see her. I got to introduce her to my father! She could only stay for a week, but I took what I could get.

Our first Thanksgiving was coming up and the kids and I were alone. We went to visitor's day and we met some nice family's in the visiting room over the months. Fred had a brainstorm to invite some of the people I met to Thanksgiving dinner. Some of them had come a long way to see their loved ones, and nowhere to go for the holiday. I agreed along with some of the single moms with kids in our complex.

Everyone pitched in, and we had a great time! I took pictures (with my Polaroid) and I took them to show Fred afterward. I was good friends with the manager of the complex. She lived next door to me She and her son were alone too. I was never so overjoyed to feel like I had true friends. My kids were happy.

Christmas was coming and there was no money for a tree or gifts. My mother-in-law sent a little extra for the kids that month. On one of my dad's visits through town, he stopped by with some gifts for me and the kids. He even brought a tree with him! We were so surprised! I loved him so much for that. I really didn't know what I was going to do for the kids. My heart was full.

A couple of days later Fred called. He never called unless it was important. He knew I couldn't afford the collect call. He said to expect a package. I didn't know what he was talking about. Apparently, there's a group called "prison ministry." They got together and sent toys for the kids. There was a huge box at my door the next day. They told us it was from Santa. They were all wrapped and had the kid's names on them. The kids were so excited and huge weight fell off my shoulders. My kids were having a Christmas! Fred called. He got a weekend pass to come home! God is good! It was the best Christmas I ever had. God never let me down.

The day came for Fred to go to the half-way house then home for good. I had told my manager my story and that Fred was coming home. She was very understanding and supported me every step of the way. I thank God for her every day. They got along so well, and he felt so welcomed by everyone. No one judged him.

Fred was a new man. It's amazing how humble you can be when God gives you a second chance. Everything seemed to fall into place. He started a small handyman business and did what he could. Not too long after Fred was home

My One True Father

for good, we got a call from Fred's sister one night. His mother had passed. Fred said his sister told him that he had to go to N.J. for the funeral. His mom had left them both a little something. She sent us plane tickets and my neighbor whom I trusted took care of the kids. We were only gone a weekend. I had never left them both. We took the money she left us and decided to go to Georgia and start over.

I had family there. My aunt May and her family lived there. I was not ready to go back to Florida where all our troubles began. Didn't know if I could hold my head up there yet. I wasn't sure if I wanted to deal with my mom. I said goodbye to my family in Texas and my grandparents were heartbroken, but they understood.

A few years passed and I seemed to have lost touch with my father. He stopped calling, and we lost touch. I sent birthday cards and Father's Day cards and Christmas cards but to no avail. There was nothing else I could do. Before we left Texas, Fred and I got remarried. It was official. I was crazy. I had married both of my husband's twice. I can't make this stuff up!

We found a nice house in Georgia and moved in and started over "again." Fred was able to get his daughter Beth for the summer. We were a family again. Dawn and Beth had been best friends since they were two and three years old. When it came time to take Beth home before school started, we got a call from her mother. She didn't want her to come home and we had to keep her.

Well this broke her heart and she thought her mother didn't want her anymore. We thought we had to take her back to Florida before school, so we took the kids to Disney for the weekend instead. We tried to make her feel better. This was the start of a new life for us. Fred started an excavation company with his inheritance and for the first time in my life I didn't have to work.

I took the kids to school and became a homeroom mom. I volunteered at school for field trips, making baked goods to raise money for whatever they needed. I had Fred Jr. with me and not in daycare. Life was good. At one point my sister Leigh who lived in Oklahoma moved in with us. She and her family stayed with us for a while.

Fred gave my brother-in-law a job. Eventually they got their own place. I would have loved for them to stay, but she had five boys in tow. It was great having my sister with me. I loved spending time with her because we were never as close as I wished we could have been.

We had long talks and I told her what mom did to me concerning my father. To my surprise she told me how mom was not so truthful to her about her father either! I was floored! She was such a country bumpkin with a very heavy country accent. She was so sweet. Concerning mom and her dad she said, "I'm ok with it, because he loved me very much and to me, he was my daddy".

He told her the story of how he became her father. She was happy that he was honest with her. She told me her story and never told anyone else. She said now "we" have something in common. I just couldn't believe that mom could just give one of her kids away! Leigh was happy and loved the simple things in life. It didn't take much to make her that way. She raised five boys and would have given her life for any of them.

She told me she never told mom how she felt about what she did to her, but she forgave her. She asked me not to say anything because she didn't want mom mad at her, especially after what happened to me. She said she came to terms with it but, the part that really hurt her was the realization that mom gave her away to a man who wasn't even blood related. He loved her and took care of her as if he was her real father.

I think she took more care of him. I still carry her secret with me. I never told mom. About a year later they moved back to Oklahoma. It was great to get to spend some time with her and share some secrets. I had no idea how those secrets would affect my life. Even though we were sisters we really didn't know each other very well. She loved the country and needed to go back. Not long after that we decided to move back to Florida.

Back to Florida

It shook me to my core to go back there, but I was going to have to face my mother again. I didn't know if I could do that. She wanted us to come down and stay with her and we could work things out, so we agreed. Mom finally told me the truth about her and my father. (her truth) I was satisfied for the time being. Mom always had an answer for everything. For peace sake I left it alone for then.

Mom still didn't like Fred, but she had to suck it up! We were with her for a few weeks and she started hinting that she wanted us out. We left, no jobs and two kids. An old friend took us in for a few months until we got on our feet. Eventually we found jobs and our own apartment. It was rough but we came through it. I didn't talk to mom for almost a year. It seems like the more I need my mom the less she was available.

By this time my daughter was in high school and my son in elementary. Dawn met the love of her life in high school, like we all do. We really liked him. His name was Greg, and he really seemed to love Dawn. Greg's parents were very hands on when it came to take the kids to school, the movies, and anything they wanted to do. They were great. I was working midnights at a local restaurant and

Fred worked in an office during the day. We all had dinner together before I went to work.

Working all night started taking its toll on me, and I didn't like it. A cook that I worked with told me he was going to a Deli in Boca and that he could get me in. I didn't know deli food and didn't know if I could do it. I tried it and we were finally making enough money.

The girls there were sure hungry and felt threatened by me. The people there were like I've never met before. Maybe I was the different one. They didn't know how to take someone who was sincere. Some of these people were like none I had ever met before. Either way I made friends with some of my customers fast. We were finally made enough money to rent a real house! I busted my butt for my job and my second year there, they made me head waitress with nothing extra for added responsibility.

The owner was very arrogant, and I no longer wanted anything to do with him or his place of business. The head waitress that worked there before me asked if I wanted to come work for her at this new place. It was another deli, but by now I knew what I was doing. I took her up on it. It was great for a while, but there was a deli guy who didn't like me. A couple of the girls would go into the bathroom with him and I wouldn't.

My One True Father

I complained to the owners, but for some reason they were afraid of him. He got away with everything! If he set your sandwich in the window and you didn't pick it up two-seconds he would push it to the ground and tell you that you had to pay for it. Then there was a cook who wanted us to call him king! People there were always fighting. I was the new girl, so they gave me the worst station. I didn't make much money. I complained to the head waitress, and she finally rotated the stations. The other girls didn't like it. I just wanted to be fair.

The deli guy had decided I was the outsider and wasn't one of them. I didn't play by his rules, so he was always trying to get me fired. This guy really pushed me to quit but by the grace of God I hung in there. The owners knew what he was doing but they didn't fire either of us. I was popular with most customers.

I thought I hated this man for how nasty, vulgar, and all-around evil he was. I prayed that God would please make this man leave me alone! Then one day this deli guy got a call at work and he buckled at the knees. His son had been murdered. My heart broke for him. I felt so bad for what happened to him and his family. No one deserved that, not even him. He was never the same again. Not long after that he retired.

One day as I got home from work my daughter was on her way to work. She worked at KFC part time after school. I noticed she had been crying.

"What's wrong," I asked sitting close to her.

"Mom I'm pregnant, and I'm so ashamed of myself. Please don't hate me!"

Immediately I held her and told her it was ok. I'm here for you, and we'll figure it out together. We both cried for what seemed to be forever. She told me a friend of hers got pregnant, and her parents disowned her. She thought I would do the same thing. I wondered if she knew me at all in that instance. I proceeded to remind her that family was the most important thing in my life. A baby was a blessing from God.

I took her to work. When I got home, I cried some more and asked God for his help! I didn't know what we were going to do! My daughter needed me, and I was going to be there for her no matter what. It wasn't going to be easy. Fred was barely working, and I was working eight to ten hours a day.

A few hours had passed, and I had calmed down a bit. I tried to figure out what we were going to do? My mind was swimming and then it hit me! I was going to be a grandmother, and I was only thirty-seven years old. Right then I got a call from our local police department. My daughter had been hurt at work! My heart sank. I asked if she was ok? I told them she was pregnant! They wouldn't go into detail. They just asked if I could come. I flew over there. As I approached the place, it was covered with cop cars and an ambulance. I asked God to please watch over her and keep her and her baby safe.

In the short amount of time I knew about the baby I was already including him in the family. I was in a panic and tried to run to her through the front doors but was stopped by police officers. I told them I got a call that my daughter had been hurt, and I needed to get to her. They took me to her. The paramedics were checking her out, and I told them she was pregnant.

She had been shot in the throat by someone in the drive thru window by a paint ball gun. She would be ok. It could have been so much worse! I held her so tight. We cried. At that moment I realized that just a few hours earlier we thought our lives would change forever. I could have lost her forever, so having a baby was a blessing compared to losing them both. Thank you, God, it made me realize that God had a better plan for us all and he saw us through it.

Nothing was more important to me than my kids! My

kids will always know how much their mother loves them and would always be there for them no matter what. I know my mother loved us, but it was implied not shown. Fred and I allowed Greg to move in with Dawn. He genuinely loved her and wanted to marry her. She wasn't having it until they graduated from high school.

Several months later my family and Greg's family and friends got together and had a huge baby shower for Dawn. They got everything they needed. We were all anxiously waiting for this child to be born. The day came. It was a Sunday morning. She was on her way to the bathroom, and her water broke. I got the call at work and I had to go home. It was mid-season at work and a very busy day.

I told my boss I was sorry, but I had to go. He knew this day was coming and wished me well. That day I became a grandmother! I couldn't believe it! I watched my first grandson come into this world. My daughter was thrilled that her momma was there. Our relationship went to a new level. Higher than I ever thought was possible. She is truly a gift from God. I cherish every second I have with her.

A few weeks later at work my boss came to me and told me he wanted to make me head waitress. I was so excited! They gave me an extra hundred dollars a week cash for my responsibility. I was not to bother them with any petty problems. I did the scheduling, stations, and anything else that came up. I got rid of the girls who got used to doing things their own way instead of my way. I did everything as fair as I thought and gave the remaining girls their days off that they wanted and their vacation days that they wanted.

The new girls I hired had to play by my rules or I had to show them the door. I had never been given free reign before, and I loved it. I had a large following of customers, and they were so good to me. If I didn't have an open table, they would wait till I did. The manager told me that I would have customers who didn't come in when it was my day off. It pays to be yourself and to treat people the way you want to be treated.

We had a cook who was after me for quite some time. Whenever I shot him down, he would have a meltdown. He would punish me in his own ways. He would put my checks at the end of the line. He put my plates on the grill until they were so hot that I burned myself grabbing them. He knew I was married, but it didn't matter to him. I gave my all to my family and my job, but he really made my job difficult.

It seems like my whole life was full of people who just want to hurt me just because they can. Some days I left work in tears. It was like I had an invisible target on my back the people were always shooting for. I would tell my bosses, and they would tell me that they would talk to him. They never did. They were afraid of him. He ruled the kitchen and it didn't help that he was an excellent cook. Life went on.

The rental house we lived in was being sold so we had to move. Dawn, Greg, and my grandson had found their own home. We found a mobile home for sale. I was so happy to finally have something of my own. The mortgage was three-hundred and fifty dollars a month and we owned the land. Hard, sometimes six or seven days a week ten hours each day. Fred was diagnosed with diabetes and started getting sick a lot. Thank God he was a vet. We got him enrolled into the local VA. They took care of him and helped him with his meds. We didn't have health insurance. Fred took advantage of his condition and said he wasn't well enough to work and that no one would hire him.

He considered himself disabled and couldn't work but he needed an office, a separate phone line, two computers, a fax machine, and a new lock on the door so our son couldn't use his computers. WHY? He was pulling one of his "BS Schemes" to get rich quick. Guess who paid for all that stuff. We had our disagreements on all the money he was spending on his "office" supplies. One day he had me fill out a form for a new credit card. This he repeated, another then another. Then when the bills started coming in. I had a fit!

We needed a lawn mower and an edger and things for the house! By this time, I had canceled all the cards with him on them. I didn't know at the time he got new cards on his own and sent them to a post office box to hide them from me. A couple of years passed, and our son was getting into trouble at school. He met new friends in the neighborhood, and they weren't the kind of friends he needed. Fred would talk to him, but when he did it was always about how to get what you wanted the easy way.

Jr. was dropping out of school and doing drugs. I was beside myself and didn't know what to do. Fred was supposed make sure he got on the bus every morning, but he was no more interested in Jr's school than Jr. was. One day I walked into Jr's room and found him with a noose around his neck. I could feel the life drain out of me! I ran over to him and pulled it off.

"What are you doing," I cried. I was so freaked out! I told his father what happened. Jr was so stoned he didn't know what was going on around him. Fred and Jr got into a fight. I was so upset. I thought they were going to hit each other. Jr finally went into his room to pack a bag. He said he was leaving. His father went out for a cigarette. Little did I know Fred had called the cops to come pick Jr up. He wanted to Baker Act him, get emergency mental health services and temporary detention for anyone who was impaired mentally.

Next thing I knew, I was sitting in the living room trying to calm down. A cop walked in my living room just as Jr was walking out with a backpack. He held my son at gunpoint. I screamed in fright. I didn't know what was going on. He yelled at my son to drop the bag slowly and turn and put his hands behind his back. Jr didn't want to do it, but I begged him. He finally complied. As they took him out in handcuffs

I looked at Fred and said, "did you do this?"

"Yes, he's out of control!"

This was forever etched in my mind. The cop said he would be released in seventy-two hours and not to worry. I never cried so much for my son. I went back to work the next day with circles around my eyes. I had a smile for everyone to see and a broken heart that no one could see. I told Fred that he needed to pay more attention to Jr. He had so much time on his hands. Neither one of them wanted to be bothered with the other.

Fred talked me into buying a new truck. I absolutely loved it. The payments were high but work really picked up.

My One True Father

I wanted something nice for a change. I was able to make the bills and the truck payments. I was so proud of myself. I figure I deserved it. I worked hard for it too. A year later Fred talked me into getting him a good used car.

I didn't know why? He didn't work and how were we going to pay for it? He ended up with a Lexus sport. He wouldn't let me drive it, but I could pay for it! I was just making ends meet with the truck and all was well. Next thing I know Fred tells me we need a new roof. A year later the AC dies.

I told Fred he needs to go find a job or loose the car. He couldn't have it all and not contribute. He said he was working on it. God only knew what he was doing at home while I was busting my butt at work. Jr. was out of school and not working, so I told him I would help him with a good used car, so he could go find a job and pay for it himself.

He agreed. Fred had to give up the Lexus. He finally agreed but wanted a new car but less expensive. By now he was getting Social Security. He had to use it to pay for his new car. He wasn't happy, but he did it.

In the meantime, Jr decided he wanted to go back to school. He went to a Vo-tech school. I paid for all his books and classes. To no avail he went there, ended up selling drugs and dropped out. The next thing I knew, he wanted to go to barber school. I signed him up for that, and it lasted a short time. He dropped out of that too.

I did the best I could to give him a head start on life. He just couldn't let go of the drug life, not even for his momma. Somehow Fred talked him into going into the Army. Jr got his GED and enrolled. He went to basic training and refused to participate. He just wanted to come home, so they sent him home. I brought him another car after he sold his first one. He finally got a job and I was a happy camper. I trusted him to make the payments because my name was on it.

I was responsible for it. He was making a lot of money and I wasn't seeing any of it. My worst nightmare again; he was dealing. He would disappear for days, and I didn't know where he was, or what he was doing. He finally told me he had been taking his friends on trips to Orlando and the keys. He was paying for it all while I was making the car payments. Fred and Jr. fought all the time over his drug habit and his actions.

The drugs were in control not him. I watched him change into this person I didn't know. Jr. kept getting in trouble with the law. Every time they saw his car, they pulled him over and checked it for drugs. He was in and out of jail and a judge finally put him in rehab. The judge said if he leaves the rehab he goes to jail for a while.

He stayed but when he was released, he went right back to his old ways. In the meantime, Fred decided he wanted a motorcycle! I said we can't afford that, and you can't ride!! Well the next year he went out and bought a motorcycle anyway. He had met an old friend he uses to know on the police department. He was a part of a motorcycle club so naturally Fred wanted to be a part of that. He started hanging out at biker bars and drinking.

Who was this man? He was someone I didn't know anymore. I asked him where's the money coming from to pay for all this. I'm not seeing any contributions towards the bills. He told me he was a part of a pyramid program and had money in an offshore account. I never heard of such a thing. I always wondered where he got the money. He was sticking to his story. I stopped asking for money, because I wanted no part of whatever he was doing.

I came home one day and there was a second bike in the driveway. I thought he had a friend over when I went in the house. I asked whose bike was in the driveway. He said "it's mine" do you like it? What?? He said that Harley Davidson gave it to him! I said why? Because you're such a nice guy? That was the straw that broke the camel's back.

I'm done! I gave him an ultimatum, me or the bikes!

He begged and pleaded with me, but I was just a cash cow for him. God knows we had no sex life and I was done! I was just working to pay for his toys, and I realized I didn't love him anymore. I was just used to thinking I couldn't do any better. He started his life over and kept me around to pay for it. This was his second childhood. I thought that I could make it work, but I felt like a looser AGAIN! I prayed and asked God what should I do? I asked Fred for a divorce. He begged me not to do this, and he cried a few crocodile tears. He had to go to a biker meeting, so he got on his bike and rode off. "We'll talk about this when he got home. I asked him to leave and I filed for divorce.

In the meantime, I had to contend with Jr. By the Grace of God, I'm here to tell my story. First thing I did was I called and canceled the credit cards. I never felt so stupid in my life! I believed in him and trusted him only to find out I didn't even know him. My trusting soul has failed me again. Taking people at their word was my downfall. The people I've loved the most hurt me the most.

Fred finally found a place to live and started to move out. Jr. came to me and asked me if I would be upset if he moved in with his father, so he could keep an eye on him. I told him if that's what he wanted to do I was ok with it. I also said if it didn't work out, he always had a home with me. The next day Jr. came home all upset, because his father told him he couldn't live with him. The apartment was for ages fifty-five and over. For a year I worked at least six days a week and went home. Sometimes I would go out with my co-workers and have dinner and a drink. My son still had some issues, but I dealt with them the best way I could.

My stepdaughter gave me the number to a divorce lawyer, and I started the process. I called Dawn and told her that I filed for divorce and that my marriage was over. To my surprise she asked, "are you sure"?

"Of course, I'm sure, Why?"

She started to cry, "I just want to make sure, because I have to tell you something that I should have told you years ago."

"Oh my God what's wrong? You know you can tell me anything!"

My sweet daughter told me that years ago Fred molested her. I said "WHAT!" I thought I would die.

"Mommy please don't be mad that I didn't tell you

sooner. I didn't want to hurt you, and it wasn't as bad as you had it when you were younger."

"That has nothing to do with it. It's not ok to touch you anywhere!"

I was upset with her for not telling me, but I couldn't stay mad at her it wasn't her fault. I called Fred and asked him, how could he? Of course, he denied it, and I immediately called the police. Even though it happened years ago, I wasn't letting it go.

I suddenly found myself in my mother's shoes. She didn't do right by her daughters, and I was going to do right by my daughter. My daughter held this in for years and didn't tell me for fear of what it would do to me. She put my feelings first, and I love her for that. I always told her it's not ok for anyone to touch her and not tell. She was afraid, and I know that fear oh so well.

The cops came and made a report. They said that probably nothing would come of it. I told them she was a minor at the time! They told me they would pick him up and ask him some questions. Because he was once a police officer, they all knew nothing would come of it. I figured I would put it in God's hands, and he would deal with him.

I felt so much anger and apologized to my daughter

over and over. How did I not know? She told me it lasted six years. It started when she was eleven, and I worked midnights. Six years was too long. Six years of me not knowing. My daughter never held it against me. I don't know what I would do if she did. She didn't want me to worry.

One night I got a call from one of Jr's friends and he told me that Jr was in a bad way. He was running up and down the middle of the street in traffic. They were afraid he might get hit by a car. He was flying high. I asked if they called the police and they said no we don't want to get into trouble".

It was two o'clock in the morning, and I had to get up at three-thirty to get ready for work. I drove out to the area where they said he was. When I got there the cops were looking for him. They had stopped traffic. A helicopter was in the air with a search light on. I was there praying that God was watching over my baby boy. They finally found him. They put him in an ambulance and took him to the hospital to pump his stomach. I followed them to make sure he was ok, but they wouldn't let me see him. He caught sight of me and started yelling. "I want my mom," he screamed. I went over to calm him down, and he hugged me and said he was sorry.

They baker acted him again. Is it bad that I was relieved to know where he was, and I had a couple of days off from worrying about him? I was at work a few hours later tired, but I had bills to pay and now a divorce to pay for too. I didn't bother to call his father. He was too busy with his new life. I called his sisters, and they were very supportive.

I finally started to save some money and I saved enough for a tummy tuck! Fred always made me feel insecure about my stretched-out tummy. I also had a hernia, so for my birthday that year I went for it. Big mistake! They almost killed me. I got a staph infection and was in the hospital for two weeks. I told my job it was a hernia surgery gone wrong.

I was embarrassed that I spent so much money on a surgery, and it almost killed me. I never told Fred. He never knew. After the divorce I rarely saw him. He started his new life with his biker buddies. I was happy not to have the added expenses he cost me. Now I could move forward.

The Dr. who performed my surgery paid for all my medical bills, because it was his fault. He thought I was going to sue him. I just wanted to feel better and not be worried about all the bills. I finally healed and put all that behind me. One day at the end of my workday I saw a guy on a motorcycle pull up in the parking lot of my job. For some reason I couldn't stop watching him. It was very strange that I was so mesmerized by him. I just couldn't stop starring at him.

I watched him as he got off his bike and proceeded to take his helmet off and walked into the restaurant. He saw me looking at him, and to my surprise came right up to me. I still didn't know who he was. He scared me, because he had on jeans, a t-shirt and tattoos all over his arms. I thought it was one of Fred's new buddies coming to say hi. I didn't know what he wanted with me! Next thing I knew he took off his sunglasses, and I immediately knew who he was! It was my old boyfriend Dick! I never forgot those bright blue eyes. I don't know how he found me, or how he knew where I worked but, there he was.

I immediately threw my arms around him and gave him a big hug. He was married but separated. He told me he had seen Fred at a biker bar, and he asked how I was doing. Fred knew Dick and I dated once upon a time. Dick also knew one of my sisters whom he worked with and asked her where I was working. That's how he found me. Fred told him we were divorced, and that's why he looked me up.

Dick was a police officer and most of the bikers they

all hung out with were all cops and retired cops. Fred's daughter Beth was not speaking to her father. They had their own issues, but she and I were ok. One day Fred came over for his mail and asked me to tell Beth to please call him. He wanted me to tell her that he loved and missed her very much. They were once very close.

My family and I were celebrating one of my grandson's birthdays. Beth and her kids were there. I went over to her and gave her a hug, and I gave her the message from her father.

"Ok," she replied and let it go.

"It's been two-years since you spoke to each other. God forbid something happens to him, and you never get to tell him you love him again, can you live with that?"

I was done and didn't bring it up again. One week later I got a call from the VA hospital. Fred had suffered a heart attack, and my name was the one to call in case of an emergency. I got there as soon as I could. He was on a breathing tube and unconscious. They told me he also threw a blood clot to the brain. He wasn't coming back from that. His brain was swelling. It was a matter of time.

I called my kids and told Dawn to call Beth. The hospital gave me his phone, and I was able to call his other daughter in North Carolina. Lynn was his oldest, and they didn't have that great of a relationship either. I told her what the Dr. had told me, and she and her mother came down right away. Upon her arrival Lynn proceeded to let the hospital know that she was the "next of kin," his oldest, and that her father and I were divorced. She was the go-to person for his care. They told her it was his wish that I was called.

They went through her not me, and I was ok with that. It didn't make me leave him alone. A couple days went by, and I took some time off work to go to the hospital. Dawn stayed with me if she could. Lynn and Beth came, some of Fred's friends came and went, but I just couldn't leave except to go home and shower and change. The Dr. called me in and told me it wouldn't be much longer.

Jr. took it hard. Even though they didn't see eye to eye, he loved his father. I knew this was going to send him into a tailspin. That afternoon after everyone left for the day. I stayed. I had ridden up with Dawn and she asked how I would be getting home. I hadn't thought about it. I just knew I couldn't leave him alone that day. After twenty-five years, off and on, through the good and the bad, I did love him once. We had a child together.

Before Dawn left, she walked over to him and with a

broken voice and tears in her eyes she said "Fred, I forgive you, and I love you." Then she really cried her eyes out. We both did. She wanted him to know before he left this earth. That night, his heart was getting weaker. I sat and talked to him for a while. I prayed for him before I started falling asleep in a very uncomfortable chair.

The nurse came in and said, you're not supposed to be here. If you want, I can take you to the nurse's lounge with a sofa you can sleep on. She added she would come get me when it was time. She didn't have to do that, but Lynn had really pissed off the nurses. They understood who I was. I knew that was going to be his last night on this earth. I couldn't leave him to die alone.

A couple of hours later a nurse came in and told me that it's a matter of time. Maybe I should call his kids. They called Lynn and I called the others. I went in to see him before the others came for the last time. I told him I loved him, and that I forgive him, and he wasn't alone. Everything that I went through with him just seemed to fall away. I laid my head on his chest, and I listened to his heartbeat for the last time. I prayed to God to please take him home. I prayed for his soul and asked God to help me with what was next.

I called one of my sisters and asked if we could have a

memorial at her church. She said yes with no problem. She took care of the church, flowers, and even food. I called the paper for an obituary with a picture and time and place for the memorial. Low and behold a full motorcycle club showed up. There was standing room only.

I saw people I hadn't seen in years. Dick showed up too! My family and I gave Fred a beautiful send off. His daughters only contributed for his cremation. The VA sent an honor guard, and the girls fought over who was getting the flag. I told them that Jr. was the only one of his kids who had anything to do with him, and he should have it. They didn't like it, but it was given to him.

Lynn, her mother, and Beth came over to Fred's apartment where Jr. was to meet us. They raided the place! Jr. was so upset and just couldn't face his father's death. He was inconsolable. It really sent him into a tailspin. I asked the girls to come over to my house. I wanted to give them a few things. They both reached out for my truck. One was their father's, and the other was mine. I told them that I talked to the car dealership where he got it. I told them that he passed, and they needed to come gets the truck. I'm sure they could have taken it over, but the payment was too expensive.

The other one I told them it was mine, and it only had

my name on it. When we went inside, I brought out some photo albums. One was of Lynn, all baby pictures, birthday pictures, etc.... She said to me, "Oh this is mine!" I said, "no it's mine, but you can have it!" I couldn't wait for her to go back to where she came from. She suddenly had that "I'm entitled" attitude, and I never saw that side of her before.

God's Kindness

Life went on. I went back to work, and my son began to experience legal problems. I did the best I could with him. I had no idea what to do, or how to do it. I met all kinds of people at my job. Some were the nicest and some were not. I was fortunate that God gave me a passive attitude with even the worst customers. It was like having to be an actress. My job was difficult, but it paid the bills for years.

One day I got the nerve to ask one of my customers, who happened to be a lawyer, if he could help me with my son and his legal problems. He told me to come to his office and we can talk about it. I went with my son, and he took our case. It cost me three-thousand dollars up front, court cost, and his driver's license was suspended. I was overwhelmed! I put everything on a credit card. I didn't have that kind of money, and I sure didn't have a savings account.

I probably should have waited on my surgery, but I wanted something for me for a change, water under the bridge now.

A good year had passed sense Fred died, and my son was still having a drug problem. I didn't know what to do for him. I just took it day by day. One day one of my regulars came in (Dale) and all the girls thought he was so good looking. He was married. I always waited on him, because he liked me. He came in and announced he left his wife and was filing for divorce. He asked me out.

I had to think about it. I didn't want to go through that again. He assured me he was looking for his own place, and he was staying with his parents for the time being. He finally came in and announced that he got his own place and asked me out again. I accepted. We had a great time and for several months it was all going great!

One day he came over unannounced, and I was happy he did until I found out why. I was crazy over him. He was there to break it off with me. I asked why? He just said, "you'll find someone who deserves you." He gave me a hug and left. I was broken hearted. I loved him, and he broke my heart. My friends decided to take me out to dinner and a few drinks and bash men. Low and behold who walks in but Dale and another woman.

What's wrong with me? I'm always trusting the wrong people!! He saw all of us and quickly went the other way. That's was the last time I saw him. Everyone at work knew this guy. They all started asking why he wasn't coming in anymore. One day I was calling my son-in-law, and the voice on the other line didn't sound like him.

"Greg" is that you?"

"No, it's me Dick."

"Oh my God! I'm so sorry I thought I was calling my son-in-law."

"No, it's me Dick, how are you? I'm divorced! Please talk to me."

I should have followed my head not my heart. I was lonely. I worked a lot, and he was divorced. Ok let's talk, let's start over. For some reason I was such a push over. I believe in people, and that they were honest. I always took them at their word. I have every reason not to trust people, but I do. Thinking people thought like I did is a bit naïve but that's how I thought. My gut instincts are usually good, but I choose not to listen sometimes, and that's when I get into trouble.

Dick and I started dating again. We were both divorced so no guilt to deal with. We dated thirty-years ago for the first time, and now it's come full circle. Wow I gave both my husband's second chances and now Dick. I'd like to think I'm older and wiser now. Our kids were grown, and we were both alone. Jr. was still my top priority. With Dick being a cop, he wanted nothing to do with my son in the shape he was in.

Jr. lived with me in a mobile home, and I was still stressed over him. Because of this I didn't always tell Dick what I was facing with my son. I worried about him every second of every day. One day Dick asked me if Jr. was his. He said the timing was right. He thought Jr. resembled him. I said "NO" he's mine. Fred and I were together two-years before he was born.

I got tired of coming home to my son and his friends hanging out not working. I told him it was time for him to move out and grow up. I've had enough. I'm going to sell the house and moving in with Dick. He didn't like it, but he had to accept it. I thought this was the only way to get him motivated. The day came when I moved in with Dick.

Day one I should have known it wasn't going to work out. I moved everything that was in boxes by myself, and with my last trip Dick was sitting in his chair watching me not once offering to help me. He said he had a bad back. I let it slide.

"You want to go get something to eat? I'm starving," I asked.

"No, I already ate," was his reply.

My One True Father

That should have been my first red flag. I finally got my stuff put away. My bedroom furniture was in a spare room. My new living set was in a huge empty living room where his furniture used to be. I guess his ex-wife took it with her. After of a couple of days there, he started to complain about the hour I got up for work, which was three in the morning. He didn't get up until six. He complained about my snoring, so I slept in the spare room when I had to work. Red flag number two. Dick talked a lot about his "Bad Ass" days all the time and I sat and listened and acted all impressed. Fred was a big talker too, so I knew how to act. I learned quickly not to question anything, because he thought I would think he was lying but he always contradicted himself. Red Flag number three.

Dick had two girls. They were very sweet and very nice to me. I got along with them very well. My son moved in with his girlfriend, and before I knew it, I was going to be a grandmother again. On our first Thanksgiving he wanted me to take time off to go away to his families for the holiday. I wasn't allowed to take time off during the season. The holidays were a very busy time for work, all the snowbirds were there, and the restaurant was very busy.

He was upset with me. He left me alone anyway and that was fine with me. The next year I traded Thanksgiving with my co-worker, so I could host dinner at our house. I made plans with my sisters, who's going to bring what, and I was so excited! I always had to work every holiday even Christmas. I never got to host a Thanksgiving. Well Dick got home from work, and I couldn't wait to tell him my good news! He wasn't too happy and started yelling at me.

What's wrong? He said I didn't ask his permission to have dinner at his house! I gave him money toward his mortgage. I paid all the utilities and groceries and I cleaned, cooked, and did his laundry. I even washed and pressed his uniforms for work. Dear God, why isn't this man happy? He was a bit of a control freak, and I had to play by his rules. He would pick fights with me if we were going to my family's house for any kind of celebration. He didn't want to go. He thought I didn't know what he was doing, but I wasn't that stupid.

He wouldn't go to church with me at night or for Christmas when my sisters were singing. We were going to one sister's for dinner, and his daughters were meeting us there, but he told them to go ahead. We'll be there soon. He was so upset because he didn't want to go. I called his daughter and told her how her father was acting, and I'd be there without him. She got so upset with him that she called her mother. She told her mom that her dad was being mean to me. She didn't know what to do about him.

My One True Father

I never told my family how he treated me. I was just, so tired of men walking all over me I was just tired of it. The summer was coming. It was June and my granddaughter was almost here. The day came and I got a call from my son. they were at the hospital. I asked Dick if he wanted to go with me. I was so excited and couldn't wait to see her. He said "no." I was happy he did. His attitude was not something I wanted to deal with that day.

I came home late, and he asked if I was there all day. Of course, I was where else would I be? He was the jealous type. He once told me that he cheated on all his wives but would never do that to me. I prayed to God for months to please take me away from this place I came to hate!

One day a regular customer of mine came in. His name was Dan, and he looked very upset. I asked him what was wrong, and he started to cry. I didn't know what to do, and all I could think to do was give him a hug. He was always alone and occasionally a friend would come in with him. He always told me stories of all his travels and the kind of people he would meet in different countries.

I had never been anywhere, and I was fascinated with all his stories. I once asked him why he never married or had children. He told me he just didn't have time. He regretted it now. Then he told me why he was so upset. He said years ago he had cancer and now it's back. It was in his vocal cords. I felt so bad for him, and I just didn't know what to say.

He kept coming in and I talked to him every day as usual. One day I asked him if he would like to go to dinner with me, and I never saw his eyes light up so fast. He said, "Really? Sure, you're alone, and in a sense so was I. I'll come and get you and we'll go out to eat." I gave him my phone number. He asked if my boyfriend was going to be upset. I said, "no." I didn't get into details I just told him it wasn't working out with him. We went to dinner, and we had a great time. The next day he came in as usual. This time he had a nurse with him. Her name was Sara. She was very nice and over the next few weeks we got to be good friends. She came in every day with him.

Dan was getting worse, but I kept taking him out a few times a week until I couldn't anymore. He was getting weaker and in and out of the hospital. Sara would call me when he was in the hospital, and I would go see him. He really appreciated my visits. He was so alone, and I just couldn't ever leave him when he needed a friend. I did in a way know how it felt to be all alone in this world. My heart truly went out to him. He used to cry in fear of dying alone, and I told him I would be there for him.

One day when he was strong enough, he came back to the restaurant. His nurse Sara went to the ladies' room. He asked me to come over to his table. "I want to ask you something."

"Ok, what is it?"

He asked me to marry him! I stepped back and said WHAT? I had no words. Finally, I said, "Dan I love you dearly, but I'm not in love with you." Then it got awkward. He apologized and I said, "I have to marry for love." We continued to be friends, and it was after our last meal together when I got the call from Sara.

Sara called me to the hospital one last time. Dan didn't want me to see him the way he was, but I went in anyway. When he saw me, he motioned me to come closer so I could hear him. I leaned over to hear him say, "I Love You." I told him I loved him too and with tears in both our eyes I kissed him on the cheek, and a few minutes later I left.

I knew that was the last time I would see my friend. I cried all the way home. I realized he was looking at a death sentence. I looked at my life, and I was just miserable. It put things in perspective for me, and I had to do something with my life. The next day Sara called me at work and said Dan was in Hospice, and he didn't want visitors. He didn't want me to see him there. I had to respect his wishes. Sara called me the next day at work and told me he died that day.

I went home from work and went out in the back yard and just sat and cried. Dick found me out there and asked what was wrong and I told him that my friend Dan died. He turned and went back inside. I expected him to show some compassion and hug me and tell me he was sorry for the loss of my friend, but I got nothing. Maybe I'm a little sensitive, but anyone with a heart would have at least said I'm sorry for your loss.

A week later a gentleman who I've seen before with Dan came into the restaurant and had an envelope for our Deli guy, one for our cashier, and one for me. He was the executor to Dan's will. He left the deli guy and the cashier five-hundred dollars each. When I opened my envelope there was a cashier's check for twenty-thousand dollars. I was floored! I've never seen a check like that before and with my name on it. I was at a loss for words and I couldn't stop crying. I went home and put it away. I didn't think it was real and one day I took it out and took it to the bank. They asked me what I wanted to do with it? I put it in an IRA. It was real. I'll never forget that a simple act of kindness can go a long way. Thank you, Jesus.

A few days after that right before I went to bed, I got a

call from my boss and he told me to call my girls and tell them not to come to work. There's been a fire at our restaurant, and we were going to be closed. I asked for how long and he said he didn't know but he would be in touch. Thankfully I had rented out my house and put the money aside. Again, God is good.

This is the time I needed to find another place to live. The spare room became my every night room and I had become a glorified roommate. I pleaded for God to take me away from there and here was my chance. I started to see what God was doing in my life. He did hear my prayers. I had to have faith, hope, love, and keep praying, and trust in the Lord.

Once Dick went to work, I spent my days looking for an apartment and finally found one. I told him I was leaving and that our relationship was over. I walked on eggshells so I wouldn't upset him. He liked to yell a lot, and this was a big fear I had because as a child, after the yelling hitting was next. He never hit me or even tried but, in my mind, that was next. In Dick's eyes I was always wrong, I guess that made him feel superior, and I just couldn't take it anymore. I never told my family about the way he treated me, I was always the weak or passive one and he knew it. I always felt like a looser and I just wanted to live in peace so I sucked it up and kept it all to myself, that way no one could criticize me and tell me how wrong I was about anything or hear an "I told you so" I took care of myself, and my kids the best I could and God was watching over me, he never left me, so knowing that, I moved forward and thanked God every day for whatever came next.

I called a moving van to come when Dick was at work and before he got home, I was safe in my own little apartment. He didn't know when it was going to happen or if it really was, he thought I was just trying to scare him. He really didn't want me to leave, he had it made and when I did leave, he wanted me back. God gave me this time to flee and the means to do it and so my prayers were answered. I knew this relationship was not for me, but after the failures I've had I wanted one to work out for me, but this one wasn't it. I asked God for a better life and God took me out of my situation and gave me some peace. Thank you, Jesus, !!! I wish I had opened my eyes to God more throughout my life, but I guess I had some lessons to learn. We all do and it's as simple as just a prayer. God does hear you and he knows your life better than you do.

I was out of work for three months, but because of my friend's generous gift, I was able to pay my rent, my bills, and pay off my truck with a few bucks from my savings account. Expect the unexpected! (In a good way) Think positive and know God is there for you. You must help yourself too, he's got your back! My son and his girlfriend were fighting, and they were both messed up and now, an innocent child was in the middle of it all.

My son came to stay in my spare room, and I was still trying to get him clean. My son's girlfriend Gina was a nice enough girl, but I didn't know her that well at the time. I tried to help them both and without anyone in my ear telling me what to do all the time, I did things my way. Well, back to work, I couldn't wait! I got a new lease on life and a new life to start. I started to work every day to keep busy and to be independent again and to answer to no one. It was hard going back to work and my son was getting worse. I would go days without seeing him. I wondered where he was and if he was ok. God I can't do this alone! I found out I had money missing, and I thought I misplaced it or miss counted, but in the back of my mind I knew the truth I just didn't want to believe it. I prayed to God that he would bring me someone who believed in him and who would go to church with me, and love me, and all my insecurities, because I know God doesn't want us to be alone. I knew his time would be right, so I waited.

One day my brother-in-law Curtis called me to see how I was doing and if there was anyone special in my life. I said no, I was in no hurry to go down that road again. I was in control and I was going to be the one making decisions in my life for once. I asked God for his help and I believed he brought me to this time in my life and I wasn't about to mess it up. A while later he called me again and said I have a perfect guy for you, and before you say anything let me tell you a little bit about him.

His name is George, he's my accountant and he's single, and he's a gentleman. He believes in God; he goes to church and he's been divorced for a few years now. He's also my friend and I've known him for a lot of years. George happened to be in China on vacation, but Curtis told him about me. He seemed to be interested and Curtis told him all about me, and he didn't run! I remember meeting him the year before when my sister Lois and I were shopping, and Curtis called and asked us to meet them for lunch.

One day to my surprise I got the courage to call George. I've never called a guy for the first time. I told him who I was, and I asked him about his trip. We seemed to get along fine. We slowly started to date, and he was a perfect gentleman. I asked God if he's the one for me I wanted him to be different, I wanted to just date and nothing else. I wondered if he could live with that until I was ready to take our relationship any farther. I wanted to be friends for a long while.

George was a lot of fun and very patient. He took me to

a lot of places, football games, basketball games, and we talked a lot. He was genuine. I slowly told him of my life but not enough to scare him away, but he already knew most of it from Curtis, and he didn't run. We both seemed to have the same goals, and we shared the same wish, to travel and see the world. After our dates he would drop me off at my door but never came in. He had two of the sweetest dogs, Baxter and Bridget.

We went out to eat a lot and one day he asked me if he could come over and make dinner for me. He cooks!! BONUS!! Of course, I said yes, and I told him I really don't like to cook, being in a restaurant all day and coming home to cook is not my thing. He was totally on board. He asked if he could bring his dogs over too. Of course! I wasn't used to someone asking me permission for anything! So, he cooked, and I cleaned. Cleaning was my thing. George never stayed to late because he knew how early I had to get up. I found myself falling for him and his dogs. He was a perfect gentleman and never pushed himself on me.

After we had been together for five or six months, we were coming home from a night out and he pulled up to my apartment and kissed me good night and for once I asked him in. He was so excited, we both were. I fell in love with this man and I prayed to God he was my forever. After that night, my nights were never alone again. He started to come over every night after work and make me dinner and stayed until I had to get up and get ready for work. He would leave at four in the morning and go home to his dogs.

He started to bring his dogs with him, and this got to be a little much on him, so he asked me to move in with him. I had to think about that because I had my son to consider. He said bring him with you! I thought that was sweet, but I was afraid that might be a deal breaker if Jr. was out of control. Jr. moved in with Gina and her family again. Her parents liked Jr. and I told George I still had a couple of months on my contract for my apartment and I would have to pay for that. I went to the office and asked if I could leave early would they make me pay for it. They said yes. I had a little more time to think about George's offer.

The next day the office to my apartment called me and said if I wanted to leave, they would let me out because they had someone who wanted a first-floor corner apartment. I couldn't believe it! Again, Thank You God! I was sure this was a sign. Time to pack. I got boxes and every day after work I would go home and pack. One day I went home and half of all my furniture was gone. I thought I was robbed, and before I could call the police, George called and said he and his son picked up my furniture and put it in storage. I was shocked!

This was the first time I didn't have to do all the work! I've never met anyone like him before. He always put me first and it felt good to be number one for a change. No one has ever done that for me, ever! We finally got settled and George wanted to take me on vacation. I was so excited, a vacation!! He asked me where I would like to go? I never thought about it, we talked about traveling but I never thought he would make my dreams come true. He gave me a choice, Alaska or Hawaii? Oh my God!! I asked him if he was serious and he said yes! He had been to both and he wanted to take me. So, our first vacation was Alaska!

I've never been so happy or felt so loved. God does answer prayers. I've never been so far away from home or my family before. I had a new life and I was happy. I had a few pieces of jewelry from my past relationships and I wanted a clean start, so I sold it all and told George I was paying for my share, I needed to contribute. We had a great time and it was so exciting to see God's creations. From that time on we decided to take a nice vacation every year. I felt like I really found favor with God this time. Everything seemed to be falling into place for me, my dreams were coming true! I already found favor with God; I just didn't see it.

Shortly after we got home my bubble burst. George decided I needed to contribute more than I already was. I didn't see that coming! He said he wanted a partner not a dependent. I was floored, I gave all I had to give and sold all my jewelry to go on this trip, so he didn't bare the whole expense. He didn't ask me to pay for my own way, I insisted. I gave what I could to help with expenses around the house, but I still had a mortgage and my own bills to pay and not to mention my son. I didn't make the money he makes but I made enough to survive. We fought for a while and I left him for about a week. That was the only thing we ever fought about at that point. One of George's friends told him "never make it about money"!! Money hasn't been an issue since. We finally got past that and my birthday was coming up and he knew how that made me feel, so he decided to take me away to San Francisco for a long weekend. For someone who fought with me over money, he got over it and put me first. I was both thankful and totally excited! Another vacation!!!

During this time my son was still having legal problems and was in a halfway house. He was absolutely determined to clean up and do something with his life. He got a job and was showing he was responsible. He no longer had a car, so he took a bus to work. He got permission from his parole officer to go to church with us every Sunday. We were all so excited to spend one morning a week together and of all places God's house! Jr. listened to every word; the preacher had his full attention. Afterwards we had time to take him to breakfast. One Sunday before the service was over, they always ask if anyone would like to give their life to Christ. To this momma's surprise my son looked at me and said "mom I got to go" my eye's teared up instantly with joy and so full of love and pride for my son and that Jesus touched his heart that day. I ask him if he wanted me to go with him. He said "no, I got this".

My heart was so full of love that day, I knew that instant that God was working in his life and everything was going to be ok. Jr. asked us if he could go to his Aunt Ann's church with her one Sunday and if she could pick him up. Of course, she did, and he did something so special that none of us expected. He asked if he could speak to the youth group about the evils of drugs and alcohol. He told them of his experiences and with tears in his eyes was thankful that God brought him through it all. If you know my son, he's the most shy and quiet soft-spoken person you'll ever meet, for him to do this and no one asked him to was a miracle. My sister said she sat in the back of the room crying and listing to every word. Then those kids started asking him questions and were genuinely interested in every word. My son sure had a lot to say that day and wanted something good to come out of the mess that was his life. Jr. wanted to make a difference and hopefully reach these kids. These kids really appreciated Jr. coming to speak to them and wanted him to come back.

Jr. is finally out of the halfway house and his father-in-law is making sure he goes to meetings. He gave my son a roof over his head and is a father figure in my son's life. My son daughter-in-law and granddaughter all live together under one roof as a family now. Thank you, Jesus,

George decided with a friend of his to purchase a small truck for Jr. George is one of those guys who has a guy for everything. If you need a plumber or an A/C guy, George has a guy. This guy owed George so he horse traded and got a deal on a small truck for Jr., but he didn't just hand it over to him like I would have. He split the cost and made Jr. give him a monthly payment until he paid it off. He taught him how to be responsible and appreciate what he had. Every car he ever had I paid for and I didn't realize how much I enabled him. I guess that's a mother's love. Between George and Jr's father-in-law taking an interest in my son, Jr. is now on his way to be a good father, husband, son, and, Christian. God put the right people in his life and I'm so thankful. Jr. still had a court date pending but all I can do is put it in God's hands. It's been a year together and Christmas is coming, we were invited to my sister's house for our annual family time. We always get together for the holidays. It's the only time we're all together under

My One True Father

the same roof.

Somewhere in time we all grew up and put our past behind us and learned to deal with our demons by putting them in God's hands. We all go to church, and we all try to look forward in life, not in the rear-view mirror. (even thou I still have issues) This was mine and George's first real Christmas together as a couple. Christmas day came and we were all together in the living room opening gifts etc.... and George suddenly stands in the middle of the room and gets everyone's attention, which is hard to do with that group, and begins his speech about how thankful he is to be there with this family, and thanked my sister for the invite to our celebration, and wondered "if this beautiful woman (pointing at me) would be my wife?? OH!!

The excitement was overwhelming, and the crowd became more alive! Everyone rushed us and hugged us, and George and I got separated in the crowed, he poked his head up from the crowd and yelled out "Did she say YES"? Another happy day this man gave me. He handed me the most stunning ring I've ever seen. I've never felt so special in my life! He's the one!

So, I assumed we would go to the justice of the peace or to Vegas to get married because George and I have both been married a couple times before and I thought it wouldn't be a big deal. I was ok with it. I never had a church wedding or a dress or a reception. None of the frills of a wedding, not even family at either of them. Well another thing my husband to be wanted to give me was a wedding I never had. We had it all. The only thing I would have liked to have was my father there to give me away. I tried but to no avail. I've sent Father's Day cards, Christmas cards, and birthday cards, but no reply. I don't know if anything is wrong but at this point, I don't know how to find out. I kind of got tired of chasing someone who obviously doesn't want to get caught. I'll try again some other time. So, I had the next best thing. My son and my only brother both gave me away. George made my dreams come true.

My son's father-in-law just so happened to own a Catering business and he hooked us up. He took care of the food, music, photographer, cake, flowers, open bar, waiters, all I had to do is pick out what I wanted. This is something I never thought I would never do in my lifetime. God has turned my life around like I never expected it to, and I realized that everything that happened to me in this life was for a reason.

Never be defined by your past, it was a lesson, not a life sentence. I still have my setbacks but I'm not alone anymore. God sent me the man I'm supposed to have, and he listens to me and understands me. I'm careful who I let in my life. I have a few people who I'm close to and know what I've been through. My own family has no idea who I am. They only see who I let them see. I'm still broken, but I'm work in progress, thank you Jesus.   Our wedding day is here, and I feel like Cinderella! Still on probation my son had to get permission to go to the wedding. For the first time in my life I was the center of attention, and in a good way!

My daughter was my Maid of Honor, my youngest grandson was the ring bearer and my niece was the flower girl. I had it all!! The ceremony was beautiful! I thought this day never existed for me. I was told after the service that George danced down the aisle. For some reason no one videotaped it! It was magic!!

Only God could make all this possible for me. God gave me a pair of strong shoulders to carry a very heavy load my whole life, and I always thought I was the forgotten stepsister and I was insignificant, all I really needed to do is give it to God. My belief in God is stronger than it's ever been in my life. We all need to go through things in life to learn not to be punished. God gives us all a freedom to choose right from wrong. It's your choice. It's your life.

The day after our wedding we were on a plane to Italy!

This was like an out of body experience, I was living someone else's life. This doesn't happen to me! We started in Rome and traveled all the way up to Venice. We stopped everywhere in between. We saw the leaning tower, the Vatican, the Coliseum Amphitheater, Niece, Monaco, we went up the Eiffel tower, and went on a gondola boat ride in Venice. We went to the Louvre in Paris and the palace in England.

These are places I've only seen on TV never dreamed I'd ever go there. I was waiting to wake up from this beautiful dream, but it was real. God made my dreams come true. George and I decided to save every penny to make this happen so it would be a true fairy tale for us.

The day we got home we found out that for some reason my son had been in jail for the two weeks we were gone for the charges pending. I thought it was all over. He had one more court date. I prayed and prayed for my son; he came so far in his journey. The day came and I sat in the court and waited for the judge to decide on my son's life. I sat and prayed so hard and the judge decided that time served was adequate, and he was free to go. Thank God! I thought my heart was going to explode with joy! If I knew he was in jail the whole time we were in Italy it would have ruined our trip.

My One True Father

Back home to start a new life as a married couple. Life was worth living. We went back to work and life was awesome. My right foot had been bothering me for quite some time, but I wasn't going to let it ruin the best part of my life. At my wedding I had to put soft slippers on because it hurt so bad.   About 9 months after our wedding I was limping around so bad in pain and I just couldn't take it anymore, so George insisted I go to an orthopedic Dr. I had to have surgery on my foot.

A simple bunion surgery trims the bone and six weeks to heal. It was a slow time at work and by the time season came around I should be ready to go back to work. The time came and I was so scared, but George never left my side. When I woke up the Dr. said unfortunately it was worse than he thought, and he had to break my foot to fix it. I thought they were going to shave a bone and sew me back up! I now have a titanium plate with five screws in my foot and eventually no more pain.

After six weeks my foot would still be swollen. I called the Dr. and he said unfortunately it might take up to a year. I needed to go back to work! I needed to be busy. George asked me if I would let him teach me how to do bookkeeping. He said give it a try. If I didn't like it, I could go back to work when I felt better. I waited tables for forty years and I didn't know how to do anything else.

Diane "Broken Arrow" Leeward

I didn't want George to think I was stupid or anything. I had no confidence in myself to try anything else, I'm too old to learn anything else. George picked up on my fears and said, "you don't give yourself any credit". Having been told your whole childhood that you were stupid and wouldn't amount to much came back to haunt me in a big way. What if Barry was right and I just wasn't smart enough to learn anything else. I was used to getting up at three-thirty in the morning and working till three in the afternoon. I did this for the last almost eighteen years. Taking it easy was not in my DNA. I was not a slacker. I was a mover and a shaker. I worked at a fast pace all my life and that's all I knew. I never worked behind a desk before. I met so many good people and close friends and it was hard not seeing them every day.

So, I tried my hand at bookkeeping. It was a slow process. I didn't know a thing about bookkeeping or accounting. I had no education for it, and I was scared, mostly my fear is that George and Fran (the girl who worked in the office) would think I was stupid. Fran worked for George for about 8 years and he taught her all about bookkeeping. He said going to school for

Accounting taught her nothing about bookkeeping so, he taught her everything he knew. I picked up on it slowly because I was also computer illiterate. (strike 2) The time came that I had to decide to go back to work or stay and become a bookkeeper in my husband's office. I struggled with it and put it in God's hands. My boss kept calling me to see when I was coming back to work. The pressure was a little hard to handle. George said he would respect whatever decision I made.

I made up my mind and went to my job and told them I was not coming back. I prayed long and hard and thought about the problems with the cooks, the disrespect the owners had for our welfare, the long hours, no holidays with my kids, and with all the years I gave them, no bonuses. The choice became easier to make. I love them dearly but when it came down to it, they were all business and "waitresses was a dime a dozen".

When I told my bosses that I wasn't coming back, there was a blank stare and neither one on them tried to change my mind or even talk me into coming back. I gave them a hug and said goodbye and I'll come visit. I came home and told George what happened, and he was happy that I was working with him. We had our ups and downs of course but we kept it separate from our home life. Any time we wanted to take time off for a weekend we could. Fran was part time, she worked 4 days a week and she kept an eye on the office while we were gone. George works very hard every day and he lives to please me. I am truly blessed. He's tough but fair. He loves and accepts my kids and grandkids. He has taken care of his family and mine with no questions. My life is truly blessed.

I got a call from my sister Lois, my sister Leigh passed away. I cried uncontrollably; our hearts were broken. We knew she was getting worse and eventually wasn't coming back from her illness. The Doctors could never pinpoint exactly what it was, but it was some form of Lou Gehrig's disease. (ALS) The few times Leigh and I could speak on the phone she was always happy. Her disease kept her from speaking for very long, so we kept it very short.

We went out to see her as often as we could but, it was only a few times before her death. When we did, she was unable to walk, talk, or do anything for herself. Her husband David did everything for her. He fed her, bathed her, dressed her, he did it all. We were very grateful he was so devoted to her. They were married for a lifetime. She was always happy to see us but frustrated that she couldn't talk to us, so we ended up playing charades until we guessed what she was trying to tell us. It was great.

We all made plans to go to the funeral, my Aunt May and my daughter also went. Dawn's father Ted lives there and it was a good time for her to see him, but the circumstances were not so good. That was the first time I had seen Ted in years. He was sad about my sister but happy to see his little girl. The service was beautiful, even the hospice nurses who took care of Leigh were there to say goodbye. We went to the cemetery after the service and we said our final goodbyes. This was very hard; it was so final. My brother Daniel was right there too and, I haven't been there in years.

This was the second sibling I've lost. We all prayed and asked God not to let her suffer and he was kind and took her home. I thanked God for the peace she found in him and it made us feel at ease with her death. We all said our goodbyes to the family we left behind there and Dawn and I said goodbye to her father. Before we left, he told me he's been married to the same woman for 20 years and he doesn't love her and how unhappy he was in his marriage. I haven't seen or spoke to him in years! Why would he tell me this? I told him he should think about going to counseling. That was the last time I spoke to him. I know he still loves me and there's nothing I can do about that. His wife even told me once that I was the love of his life and he still loved me. What is wrong with these people?

I pray he finds peace and that he and his wife can work things out. I'm glad we live a world apart and he never had my phone number. A couple of days after we got home, just like my brother, my sister Leigh came to me in a vision or a dream. She let me know she was ok. She was happy, healthy, talking, laughing, and most of all she was with our brother Daniel. I woke up and I knew this was real. I thanked God right away for giving conformation just like he did with Daniel. I know they're together in a better place. I told them to save me a spot!

We have been trying to keep in touch with David to see how he was coping without Leigh and we could tell he wasn't doing so well. He died 3 months later of a broken heart. Our hearts went out for our nephews. They've lost both their parents within a matter of months. In my spare time I like to gather family pictures together and put the all together in photo albums. I have hundreds of them. One day I was looking at my wedding album and thought about my father and what ever became of him.

I made extra copies of wedding photos and decided to send them to my dad so he could see that the kids and I were doing fine, and I hope he was too. I really wanted to reconnect with him again. So many years have come and gone, and we've lost so much time. I don't know what happened between us but, I'd like us to be close again like we once were.

I sent the pictures with a long letter hoping to see him again soon and told him all about my new life and how the kids were and about his grandkids. I sent my address, e-mail, phone number and anything else I could think of so he could get in touch with me but, I never heard back from him. He did keep the pictures; they were not returned. A few months later I got a call from back home in Texas, one of my uncles had passed. I tried to call my mother, but she wasn't home, and I thought I better go give her the bad news about her brother in person. I also called my sisters to let them know. My mom Lois and Aunt May and I made plans to go. I couldn't believe another family funeral.

It was very sad, but I did get to reconnect with cousins that I was so close to as a child and it was as if we were never separated. We laughed and joked around like when we were kids. I saw cousins I knew were family, but we were strangers, we knew about each other but didn't grow up together. I was sure I would see my father there because he and my uncle grew up together, they were like brothers as kids, their parents were married!

Where was he? At least my dad's sister, Aunt Linda met us there. I hadn't seen her in years. I've known her my whole life I just didn't know she was my Aunt. I asked her about my dad, and she said they weren't on speaking terms but, maybe because my mother and my brother Neil were there and that was a lot of bad blood there.

I'm still trying to figure out what happened? What did I do? Why? Almost a year after my uncle died, George and I decided to tour Texas. I made the mistake of telling mom we were going to visit Texas and stopping to see my dad and introduce him to George. Out of the blue she proceeded to tell me how she never wanted to tell me this but now she must. What? What now mom? Your father raped me! Just when I thought she was done hurting me, lying to me, and saying hurtful things to cover her tracks and to keep me from my father. This was the cherry on top.

Now, being a survivor of years of molestation from my mother's husband, I'm the last one to doubt a rape victim but, my mother is the world's biggest narcissist. I asked her why to tell me this now? Why? when I'm going to visit him? Another attempt to keep me away from him and make herself look like a victim? Again? Really mom!! I swear she's so afraid my siblings are going to find out what kind of mother we really have. I don't even know who she is!

Well that didn't work, and she never brought it up again. George and I went to Texas anyway, he had never really been there, and he wanted to go to Austin for good BBQ. So, we went to Austin, San Antonio, and a trip to Carlsbad Caverns. He wanted to see where my dad took me and the kids so many years ago. My Aunt Linda lived right in the middle of all the places we wanted to go, so I called her to see if it was ok if we could come see her. She was so excited and couldn't wait to meet George.

George had never met any of my family out there and he was excited to meet her. I told George that my father lived in the same town, but I haven't heard from him in years, but it wasn't for a lack of trying. I was hesitant because we became strangers over the years, and I didn't know what was going on in his life.

I decided to look up my niece on Facebook®. She was all grown up and a mother herself. I told her who I was, and I wanted to come and see them all. I was so excited! Apparently to my surprise and hers my father and my sister didn't tell her much about me. She was apprehensive and she asked me what makes me think her grandfather is my father?

I was stunned for a moment and I said both he and my mother admitted it to me years ago. Ask your grandmother. She said she didn't believe it and I must be mistaken. I could hear her getting information from her mother now because she asked me things that only my sister would ask. She asked me if I would submit to a DNA? I said of course! She said, "I saw the pictures you sent of your wedding." You have a very nice family.

She was trying to be nice but at the same time she

couldn't go against her family and she only knew what she was told by her mother who didn't like me from day 1. I didn't blame her; I was a stranger. I get it. I was also crushed. I tried to explain things to her, but she said that she was told that her uncle (dad's brother) was my father.

WHAT?? She said that her grandfather told her that. Why would he do that? She said I believe him over you. I was devastated and heartbroken and just besides myself. Why would this man who couldn't wait to get to know me decide to toss me to the curb with no explanation? Dear God in heaven what went wrong? What did I do? He wouldn't even talk to me. I looked at my Aunt and she said I bet his wife and his daughter are behind this. I don't understand. I didn't have a problem with his wife before. I guess over the year's things changed. George took my aunt and I out to dinner while we were there for only a couple of days and we ended up going into a restaurant where my half- sister and her granddaughter were sitting.

I wasn't quite sure it was her; it had been so long sense I last saw her and my aunt had her back to her so Aunt Linda turned and said Yep! That's her! I couldn't help but stare. I wondered what makes her tic. Why did she see me as a threat? I didn't want anything but to see my father for a short time and go home. She saw me looking at her and she acted like she didn't see us so, I left her alone. I'm not one for confrontation or arguing with anyone. It's not who I am unless I'm backed into a corner or someone is messing with my kids.

I just wanted to go back to our hotel room and cry. I got ahold of my niece again and told her I saw her mother and she said that my aunt and my dad didn't get along and that I shouldn't believe anything she said. She said my Aunt was a liar but, dad was lying to me! My Aunt had been trying to fill in a lot of spaces that were missing from my life. She told me about my family that I didn't know and grandparents that I wish I knew. I found out that my dad's mother was 100% Apache Indian! Mom told me my father was Irish. When I was a kid people use to ask me what nationality I was I would say Mexican and Irish. Boy when I think about it now. What was my mother thinking? People probably use to laugh behind my back. My mother made such a fool out of us just to protect her secret. I think about my dad a lot and I pray for him every day. I ask God to please help me to understand why he wants nothing to do with me anymore.

A year or so has passed and it's Christmas time so I thought I would reach out to dad again. I couldn't let go. He was like a scab I had to pick. My life was finally awesome God is good and I wanted my dad in my life again. So, I sent him a Christmas card again. When he got it, he called me! I looked at my caller ID and I looked at George and, in my excitement, I screamed "it's my dad" he's calling me!! He called me to ask me to leave him alone and that he wasn't my father. I could feel the life drain out of my soul that very second. I was devastated! Why would you say that? Why are you and my mother out to hurt me? What have I done to you? You sought me out all those years and begged my forgiveness and you loved me and my twin and my kids! I never cried so much.

He said my brother Tim is your father! I said the one who is dead? The one who kept you informed of me and my brother growing up and telling you when I needed you? Now he's dead and not to mention he was married to my mom's sister? That brother? I told him he's just as bad as my mother! Why was he so afraid of me? What did he and his family think I could do to them? It's been years!!

Everyone back home knew about him and my mother, it was no secret, but my brother and I were (so they thought). That was the last time I spoke to my father. I don't understand why God would give me a father just to take him away. Summertime was coming and I got a call from my cousin Eric. Eric is my Uncle Tim's son. Eric is aware of my father's claims and he hasn't spoken to him sense. He is quite upset that my father would disrespect his father like that. His own brother! Especially when he's not here to speak for himself. My cousin loves me no matter what and he still wants me in his life, and we decided that's what we're going to do. He called to let me know that there's going to be a family reunion on the 4th of July weekend and invited us to come and he wanted to meet George.

Diane "Broken Arrow" Leeward

My One True Father

My Turnaround

At first, I didn't want to go because I didn't know all those people, and my cousin said neither do I. Well, George was so excited, he wanted to see the small town I grew up in and the little house that my grandmother raised us in. After all these years it's still standing. My Uncle Ray still lives there. I told him yes and he was so excited, just like when we were kids. When we saw each other at my Uncles funeral a couple years back I never thought I'd see him again so soon. Reconnecting with my Texas roots was so special to me and I just wanted to go back to where the memories of my grandmother were still alive and well in that small town. All my cousins, Aunts, and Uncles were excited to see us. This was a happy occasion to go back home to. My Aunt Linda came, and we rented her a hotel room next to ours, so we got a chance to visit with her too. I met so many nice people and we all had the best time ever! Some older people thought I was my mother. I saw a little old lady, short and round just like my grandma. I couldn't keep my eyes off her. The closer I got to her the more she looked like her. I started crying uncontrollably and George and Eric asked me what was wrong I said she looks just like grandma! A cousin of my mother's told me she was my grandma's cousin, that's why she looks so much like her.

They introduced me to her, she knew who my mother and grandmother was, and she hugged me, and I just had to hold her and cry. She understood. It felt like grandma was holding me one more time and I couldn't let go. That made the whole trip even better.

I decided to take a DNA with Ancestry because I now knew I wasn't Irish. I wanted to know my full Ethnicity. Where I came from, who I really was. Now I know who I looked like every time I looked in the mirror. I am thirty-nine percent Native American thirty-four percent Iberian (Spain) eight percent Europe South and four percent Asia Central. All my life I've had an infatuation with Native American things.

My whole house is Native American!! My kids were so amazed at my findings that they did it too. I gave them the history of their fathers and to my surprise they took after their fathers more than me. They are seventeen and eighteen percent Native American. My daughter was a little disappointed, she loves the native history like I do. I was totally elated!! I knew I had Native blood in me but, I didn't think that it was that much! NO IRISH!

I called my cousin Terri and told her what I did, and she thought it was so cool and she decided to do the same thing. I couldn't wait for her to get her results because that would tell us if we were sisters or cousins. She finally texted me her results. We are first cousins! Just like we have always thought. I sent my dad the results but, he never answered. I found out later that another Aunt on my dad's side did Ancestry DNA years before and she and I were more a match than my cousin and me. I look nothing like my uncle, but I look just like my dad.

I got a call from my daughter one night and she was all upset. She asked if she could give my phone number to her father. He always asked her for it, but she never gave it to him. She told him "mom is happy now leave her alone". This was the first time she said he doesn't want to call you; he wants to text you. For some reason I said yes.

My instincts are almost always right, and this was one of those times that I had to listen. Something just didn't sound right, and she was really worried about her father. I got a text from Ted and he said he didn't think he could go on with this. With what? I asked. He said, "I don't know, was I an ass back when we were together or have, I just become that way"? I told him that was a long time ago.

Why can't you let the past go? It was over twenty years ago! Why can't you be happy? He said he wasn't sure how to be happy anymore. He didn't love his wife anymore, he tried. I told him he needed to go to counseling with his wife. I'm not the one he needs to be talking to about this. He said he doesn't believe in church stuff anymore and I told him that's why he's unhappy. Ted gave up a good job 3 months ago, he's drinking a lot, and he's depressed.

Dawn told me he was on anti- depressants. He had too much time on his hands and that wasn't good. I told him to stop scaring his daughter and go get his job back. He said he tried but just didn't know if he really wanted to. I asked him what he meant by that and where was his wife? He said he didn't want Dawn to feel bad, so he was going to leave her alone. That's not what she wants! She wants her daddy!! Dawn told me every time she spoke to Ted; he was so drunk he didn't even remember talking to her. So, talking to him was not a happy experience for her anymore. It really broke her heart. She really loves her dad.

I told Ted to try calling his daughter when he was sober. He said your right and I'm sorry. I knew in my heart what he was thinking, and it wasn't good. Dawn tried calling him and her stepmother and no answer. Dawn was thinking the same thing and I called her and told her to call the local police and have them do a wellness check. Our fears were confirmed by a single phone call.

My baby girl called me crying her eyes out, mommy my daddy is gone! I had no idea what he had been going through in his life and a few texts weren't going to help him. Now I had to pick up the pieces of my little girls' heart. She was shattered. I was so upset that he put her through this but at the same time my heart ached for him too. I can't believe his wife didn't see this coming.

This man was my first love and first of many things. I loved him dearly and he will truly be missed. We were so young and went through so many firsts in our young lives together and neither of us knew what we were doing but, the love you give to your first love, it doesn't die. I've never seen my daughter like this before.

We cried together many times and I wish I could have taken her pain away. Time and prayers and her momma are what she needs. I told her she needs to ask God to take care of him. He needed help and it wasn't his fault. Holding her in my arms and comforting her is all I could do. She made arraignments to go the funeral and the day after the funeral, we were scheduled to go to my grandson's graduation from the Navel School.

Dawn flew home hours after she said goodbye to her dad. My poor baby was a wreck, and to top it off I broke my wrist the same day as the funeral. I didn't want to tell her until she saw me because when she saw me, she panicked. She worries about me a lot. Dawn and Greg drove us to

South Carolina for the graduation. Despite everything we tried to have a good time. This was a proud time for my grandson. There's no pain greater than to see your child in pain. A few years have passed and I'm still dealing with my dad and my daughter dealing with her father's death. All I can tell her is to pray and ask God to have mercy on his soul. He was sick and he needed help. It's not her fault.

It made me think of my father and how angry I was at him, so I reached out and sent him a final letter to let him know that I'm over being angry and that I forgive him for breaking my heart. I don't know why he did it or what could have possibly happened to make him do it but, I wasn't the cause. He was so happy to be my father and ready to tell the world about me and I was so happy I finally had a daddy who loved me and wanted me for me! I told him that I just hoped that he makes things right with God before he leaves this earth because he can't lie to God about me and I said goodbye.

Well turns out less than a year later my Aunt told me that my father had cancer. He traveled to another one of my Aunts to have surgery at a better hospital and he stayed at her house till he could travel back home again. They thought the Dr's got it all, but it had traveled. He waited too long to go to the Dr. He started Chemo and it made him so sick that he decided not to continue it. He wants to have his last days not to be sick. I want to go see him but, I don't want to upset him and his family. They're already mourning him, and family is pouring in to see him while he's still here.

My Aunt and a cousin of mine are keeping me informed of what's going on. Mom caught wind of dad's condition and wants to know how he's doing every time I talk to her. I don't know why she wants to know or why she cares. My Aunt Linda called me one day to give me an update about my dad, she must go through her son because she and my dad haven't gotten along in a long time. (Another long story) He's getting worse and I can't even go see him to say goodbye. She also said that she thinks she knows why he denied me.

What? Why? She said apparently, he and his wife have money and are afraid I might want to go after that. That's the last thing I would ever want from him and his family. I never asked for anything from him when I was alone with 2 small children and no home and I never have and never will. It's hard to believe he would cut me and my kids and his grandkids out of his life for the sake of MONEY! It does make the only sense that I can think of. His excuse is lame. God forgive him. That scab I picked just started bleeding again, will I ever learn?

My sister Lois lives close to me and we're seven years apart. We didn't really grow up together, I left home just short of eighteen and she was eleven. She was always a very little girl and a very beautiful woman. She always knew what she wanted and went for it. She's a strong-willed woman just like the rest of my sisters. I was always different. I let everyone walk all over me. I was the passive one. I always wished I was like them but, I was just always afraid of my own shadow. Barry did that to me, and mom let him.

Lois and I were talking about fathers one day and she blurted out how she made mom tell her about who her real father was and how she tried to find him with no luck. She thought he might be dead. She said we all have a form of PTSD and we should see a therapist! To her surprise I told her I already was. She has a bit of a mouth on her and a bit of a narcissist just like my mother. If things don't go her way you will feel her wrath. I stay away from her and my mother these days.

A simple conversation can turn into a real bad car accident very quickly and of course it's always my fault. There comes a time in your life when you just must walk away from all the drama and people who create it. I'm not missed, no one calls me, and I don't call anyone. My brother Neil is more messed up than us all put together. He keeps asking mom who his father is, and she won't tell him. He thinks he was switched at birth or he was adopted. I believe he is still my father's son.

My sister Ann is the only one left that mom is lying to. She thinks her father is the Irishman in Indiana who still thinks mom gave him 4 kids. My sister follows mom around like a lost puppy. She is the last one on the hook. Mom uses her for everything. Lois is willing to hire a landscaper for mom's yard and a maid to take care of mom's house and to take her to Dr. appointments, grocery shopping, and whatever else she may need but, mom wants Ann to do it. Ann has a full-time stressful job, she's in her 60's she does a lot of community service for her church and Ann and her husband must go mow mom's yard on her day off.

My youngest sister Marie really got a double whammy! A narcissistic mother and a pedophile for a father. Neither wanted to be bothered with her unless it was for their advantage. I was gone and I wish I could have taken her with me, but I was a mess myself. She really distanced herself from the family and she gets criticized for it. I really don't blame her, and I do call her and talk to her every now and then. She really appreciates it and thanks me for not interfering in her life. She deserves to live in peace, and she has protected her kids from all this evil that was her life. I love this little girl with all my heart and, my heart goes out to her and I would do anything for her if I could make her life easier, she deserves to be loved and made special and she is. She has fought for everything in her life and, I do understand how she feels towards our mother and I tell her she's not alone. She knows she can call me any time for anything.

Mom is alone because she chooses to be. She doesn't want to join any senior programs and her kids (at least 3) can't be around her. If you disagree with her, you're being disrespectful. She demands respect! That's something I no longer have for her and trust is another. God knows I love her, and I forgive her, that doesn't mean I'm going to let her walk all over me and lie to me just like she has my whole life. I don't even know who she is. I pray she asks God for forgiveness too. I haven't spoken to her for a long time and I'm at peace. I often wonder to myself, when mom is gone, will I be sorry I didn't speak to her while she was still here?

The answer is a tough one but, it would still be the same ole story from mom. Mom is always the hero or the victim, I will always love her and miss her and forgive her. Mom is an extremely self-centered person who commands attention in a group, and she has an exaggerated sense of self-importance above anyone else. She doesn't seem to have emotional closeness to anyone who doesn't put her first.

Growing up she lacked in love and empathy.

Now a day discussing life issues she always diverts the discussion to herself. She always had to top whatever you're going through to satisfy her own ego and you can't help but tell her "Mom this isn't about you!" Mom always made me feel stupid and helpless in her presence and I should always do what she told me to because she knew better. Conversations always ended up about her.

She's not the perfect mother or even person that she tells everyone she is. I haven't talked to her very much in the last year and I found out that with God's help I'm stronger than I thought. She took away my choices as a child and my innocence of childhood is irreplaceable, my life was a lie, and it was altered to save her reputation but, God put me through this for a reason, so this is my story.

I know there are millions of you going through the same thing, some worse than others. Trust in God! He's the answer. You have a story to tell!! My story is about what God brought me through and he can do the same for you. Despite whatever life throws at you God will bring you through it! I sent both my parents a letter forgiving them, and I told them I still loved them but, I just can't subject myself to the hurt and pain they've both caused me. They're in God's hands now. My sanity is literally at stake. I learned the hard way that life isn't fair but, the love of God will never fail you.

God is "My One True Father" Let him be yours too!

The abuse? NO MAS!!

Appendix

This is a short note for those who think I'm disrespecting my mother. Well, I'm not. I'm trying to do the best I can to go on with my life after the life changing mess she put me in with my father. Unless you've been in my shoes, you won't understand. God put me here for a reason and getting this message out to people like me in the same situation, I feel, is now my responsibility. So, I sent this letter to my mother.

Dear Mom,

This is the hardest letter I've ever written. For many years I've been trying to figure out my life without your help. You have lied to me and my siblings our whole lives. I know Ann's the only one left in the dark with all this. She's going to be so broken hearted when she learns the truth about her real father.

Daniel isn't her father any more than Neil, Jr, or me. I wanted to know who my real father was when I was very young but, you kept it to yourself. You robbed us all not just of our fathers but, extended family, grandparents, cousins, Aunts and Uncles! I've known for 30 some odd years and I never asked you about it again. I still was the dutiful daughter. I was always there for you along with my siblings for whatever you needed.

Now you need to be honest with us. You have manipulated us our whole lives. Leigh knew the truth years ago and told me all about it when she and her family lived with us in Georgia. Lois told me that she confronted you about her father and you gave her a phony name until Aunt May told her the truth. Last time I spoke to Neil (years ago) he was out of his mind with wonder.

That's probably why he doesn't talk to you and you told us simply "I don't know why he doesn't talk to me!" I want to be set free!! One lie always lead to another with you and a lifelong secret of yours has turned into a flesh-eating bacterium for me. I started losing myself a little at a time! I wasn't good enough for anyone because I didn't know how to have a relationship or how to have a mind of my own. Everything you ever told me I believed, and I listened to you when you told me what to do. Your lies have turned my life into a black hole.

Everything changed when I left Ted. You wanted to control my life so bad and I didn't listen to you and that decision led me to my father, your worst fear. So many unanswered questions! I love you mom but, just trusting your explanations isn't an option for me anymore. You always come up like the victim you're not. You fed us to a wolf, and you looked the other way, you cared more about him than your own kids.

We never got hugs or kisses or even and I love you! We've been physically, emotionally, and sexually abused and you did nothing except come up with an explanation. Just ask my sisters, we've talked about it. We don't go to you with this kind of stuff because you redirect the conversation to suit yourself. Mom, your past now haunts me, and my struggles are real! I'm numb, angry, and feel so betrayed by you that I can't bring myself to speak to you. That's not how I want to feel about my own mother!

You once told me that my father "took you" do you know what that did to me?? You opened a whole can of worms! Suddenly my brother and I were a product of "rape"!! What am I supposed to do with that? You went through a lot of lies to cover yourself, and that one really showed me just how selfish you really are. I at least got to know my father enough to know you were lying.

How could you tell me something like that?? My poor brother is an emotional wreck and that's on you. One day I will tell him the truth, right now he couldn't handle it. You owe him that! I live with a difficult truth while you live a comfortable lie. How do you sleep knowing what you've done to your kids? You know in your heart that everything I've told you is God's truth, and my feelings are valid. This is your responsibility to fix!

I know you're going to be angry and that's ok, truth always hurts in your case. Sticks and stones can break bones but, words can never hurt, except when they do. You see yourself as a perfect mother but, none of us are perfect. We've all kept our true feelings hid deep inside and tried to show you love and respect but, you make it hard. Mom, it's never too late to make things right with your kids. My father hurt me too! I wrote him a letter a year ago to let him know that I forgive him before the good Lord decides to take one of us home.

Now I've learned he's got terminal cancer. I did right by him and you to let you know I forgive you too, I just can't be around you pretending everything is ok. I'm not that good an actress. I don't know what I did to you guys to put me through the emotional roller coaster that I've been on but, I'm done!! I've given it to God and I'm in his care now. Don't take your secrets with you mom, do the right thing!

God will forgive you and so will your kids. You've seen the pain in us but, not the hidden pain we all have. Feel free to keep this letter and re-read it till you feel it! Show it to my sisters or destroy it, I don't care anymore. I'm going to live my life with my head held high without shame! Now I got it off my chest, why don't you do the same?

I love you mom, God bless you. Now I can slowly be the person I always should have been my whole life. It's like I've been going through a grieving process and time will heal but, it's a process. The fact that I haven't dealt with it all these years is probably why I'm not "getting over it" I'm getting help from God almighty and seeing a therapist, my siblings should do the same, you've seen what it's done to them too.

Always in my heart and in my thoughts
God Bless You Mom
Love, Diane

Diane "Broken Arrow" Leeward

www.ingramcontent.com/pod-product-compliance
Lightning Source LLC
Chambersburg PA
CBHW030328100526
44592CB00010B/610